HARBOR HOME

Praise for

HARBOR HOME

As comforting and life-giving as the ocean breeze, Teresa's words will inspire you to create a home filled with wisdom and safety. Her well-told stories linger like a conversation with a good friend. The spiritual foundation for the principles offered in the book are as timeless, powerful, and authentic as the sea itself. Pick up a copy and join the cove lifestyle.

—**Marianne Hering**, former senior editor of Focus on the Family magazine

Harbor Home is a welcome book full of encouragement and ideas for creating a safe harbor in your home. It is a book I wish I had had when my children were young. It is full of useful and practical wisdom and concrete steps that you can take to create your own Harbor Home. While directed at parents, the content is beneficial for grandparents, teachers, and others that work with children. Children need a safe place to learn, explore, and develop. *Harbor Home* gives you the tools to create this.

—**Connie Ferguson,** B.S., M.S., retired special education teacher and administrator, published educational researcher, two-term president of the Texas Association of Parents and Teachers of the Deaf

In our fast-paced world, *Harbor Home* prescribes peace for readers, particularly parents—a space to sit back and think. To plan. Teresa Auten expertly uses the coast of North Carolina and all that it encompasses to weave faith-filled recommendations and encouragement together for weary parents. My favorite part of the message within is that our Harbor Homes are customized, uniquely created by us and for our own families. Teresa paints a picture where comparison, stress, and over-scheduled lives have no place. Rather our Harbor Homes should be filled with faith, fellowship, and joy. The sea is where we can all look to create meaningful lives and love-filled homes worth protecting. Thank you, Teresa, for reminding us that we have choices in our homes!

—**Cortney Donelson,** ghostwriter, co-founder of *GirlStory* Magazine, author of *Clay Jar Cracked: When We're Broken But Not Shattered,* and co-author of *The Outlier's Choice: Why Living an Uncomfortable Life is Worth It*

Teresa Auten's *Harbor Home* is a practical, Christian-based guide for families from all backgrounds. Her expertise in educating families and young children is evident and easily understandable in the unique way she connects real-life experiences, ideals, and values to the distinctive characteristics of an ocean harbor. I highly recommend this book to anyone who is looking for guidance on their journey through parenthood!

—**Kirstie Burleson,** B.S. in child and family development, NC-certified birth–kindergarten and special education teacher

HARBOR HOME

Create a Home Where You and Your Children Can Thrive

TERESA AUTEN

NASHVILLE

NEW YORK • LONDON • MELBOURNE • VANCOUVER

HARBOR HOME

Create a Home Where You and Your Children Can Thrive

Published in New York, New York, by Morgan James Publishing. Morgan James is a trademark of Morgan James, LLC. www.MorganJamesPublishing.com

Proudly distributed by Ingram Publisher Services.

ISBN 978-1-63195-728-4 paperback
ISBN 978-1-63195-729-1 ebook
Library of Congress Control Number: 2021914932

Cover Design by:
Megan Dillon
megan@creativeninjadesigns.com

Dedicated to my husband Rick, who supported this project and is my true soulmate, and to Courtney and Christian, who showed me the way to the Harbor. To God be the glory for the gift of His son Jesus.

CONTENTS

ACKNOWLEDGMENTS

I would like to acknowledge the overwhelming support of family and friends who encouraged me as this book came to life:

To my husband Rick, you are the finest man I have ever known. I see Christ in you each and every day. Your ability to love people astounds me, and the twinkle in your eyes makes me smile. The road of ministry has been filled with joy and hardship, but sharing it with you has made this journey truly incredible. Your love is the component that sustains me. 9464–777.

To Courtney and Christian, thank you for giving me the privilege of being your mother. You made it fun and exciting, forcing me to use all my creative skills and invent some new ones. I'm so proud that two such noble and generous people call me Mom. You have expanded our family in the most beautiful ways, and by bringing Erica and Jacob into the fold, you have made us look really good. We are forever grateful. To put the icing on top, you gave us Paul and Ella, Jonah, Rachel, and Kennedy. Our harbor is overflowing with wonder, and it began with you two.

Jonathan and Christina, you gave me a brand new hat to wear, and I love it. Thanks for being kind when it was hard and for welcoming me into your Harbor. Sheli and Jim, you are wonderful friends and I admire you both so much. Thanks for bringing Dylan, Lucas, Elijah, and Lillie to us. I love you all more than you can know.

Very sincere thanks to my sister-in-law, Connie, who freely gave help with early edits and supportive comments throughout the process. Also to my sister-in-law, Charlotte, my friend since I was ten, who allowed me a bird's'-eye view into her Harbor Home for decades. These two sisters taught me so much about being a Christian woman of substance. The godly influence that they had on my life cannot be expressed in a few words. Thank you for being my lighthouses.

To my formatter, proofreader, and fellow North Carolinian, Cortney Donelson, thanks for working so hard to help my story find its voice. I pray that the Lord allows this partnership to continue to grow.

To the good people at Morgan James Publishing, you believed in this book and convinced me to believe in it too. Thank you for everything.

To the people at Hope of Mooresville for being amazing cheerleaders along the way. I will never stop being grateful for the warm welcome that you offered from the moment we all met.

Thanks be to God who saves and sustains, cares and corrects. Your thoughts and ways are unfathomable. For the gift of Your Son I have no gift to return, so I give You my heart.

Introduction

THE BECKONING HARBOR

Off the coast of North Carolina lies a stretch of barrier islands known as the Outer Banks. The banks are little more than sandbars breaching the surface of the Atlantic Ocean while the Albemarle and Pamlico Sounds flank their western boundary. Those who have discovered the magic of this coastline return year after year to enjoy the natural beauty and isolation.

Fishermen and other seafarers who traverse these waters call them The Graveyard of the Atlantic. There are good reasons for this. The enormous numbers of shipwrecks lying on the seafloor testify to the ever-changing shoals and channels that have menaced ships at sea for centuries. It is here that the Labrador Current collides with the Gulf Stream creating a chaotic, unpredictable expanse of churning seas.

Amid these treacherous waters and precariously balanced threads of land, there is a small island that is the permanent home to fewer than 1,000 people. Due to the beautiful beaches, charming village, and unique atmosphere, visitors come in droves to cycle or stroll along the back roads and enjoy the shops and restaurants. It is Ocracoke Island, and it is only accessible by private boat or the state-run ferry.

How did an isolated speck in this dangerous part of the Atlantic Ocean ever become populated at all, let alone a haven for tourists and residents? The answers, of course, are complicated and vary depending on who is telling the story, but all agree on one fundamental fact: Ocracoke Island has a safe deep water harbor. It is large and deep and has a history of great importance for naval defense since colonial times. Infrastructure left behind from the naval base built here for World War II can still be identified and the American Civil War was brought to these shores as well.

The harbor at Ocracoke provides sanctuary to fishermen, sailors, itinerant pleasure cruisers, scuba divers, and all manner of boaters today as it has done for centuries. Even the notorious pirate Black Beard famously sought refuge here before he was caught and killed in November of 1718 by British naval forces in the waters surrounding Ocracoke Island.

Ocracoke's harbor, called Silver Lake, has a sheltered cove that curves generously into the island providing a substantial land barrier from the wind and waves. The ocean floor drops away at this point providing deep water with room for very large boats to come in without running aground. Many boats are moored there, and they rock quietly, even as offshore waters are too rough to safely navigate.

Ocracoke also has a feature that is rare on the Outer Banks: a deep and stable inlet that allows safe passage from the travel lanes of the ocean into the shelter of the harbor. Year after year the Ocracoke Inlet remains; it is consistent and dependable. It has remained virtually unchanged for centuries. Mariners can depend on the Ocracoke Inlet to accommodate the boats that enter the harbor from the ocean.

Hatteras Inlet, only eighteen miles northeast of Ocracoke, provides access to another harbor and some villages along the banks. But in stark contrast to Ocracoke, Hatteras inlet is treacherous, unreliable, and challenging for even experienced boaters to navigate. The channel, a ditch in the seafloor in which the water is deep enough for boats to travel, is not predictable and is sometimes barely even there. The safe route that you passed through six months ago may be far too shallow today. The intense movement of the waters shifts the sand almost constantly making the crossing of this inlet a challenging endeavor.

The harbor at Ocracoke Island has a charming white lighthouse that shines out on the ocean. During the day the fat, round, white structure with its off-set light gleams on the shore and can be seen and recognized for fourteen miles. By night its steady light marks the harbor and beckons all to safety. Tourists love to walk along the wood sidewalk past the lightkeepers' houses and just look at this small but mighty light. The structure is not open, nor are any of the houses on the light station property, but it still attracts visitors. There is something about a lighthouse that seems secure and reliable. Steady. Unchanging. Safe.

So what do all of these facts, as interesting as they are, have to do with creating the home life you have always wanted? The answer is simple: God desires our homes to be like harbors. God yearns for our families to find protection and safety from the chaos and danger of the surrounding culture within the harbor of our homes. Home should be a place in which shelter from the storm outside is assured. Although harbors are influenced by the dangerous currents and storms beyond, they remain a place of relative safety.

The same is true in a Harbor Home. There is awareness of the chaotic culture outside your door, but a Harbor Home is not changed by it. A Harbor Home can be compared to a working harbor such as the one at Silver Lake on Ocracoke Island, North Carolina.

Think about what it is that attracts mariners from the far ends of the ocean to this and other deepwater harbors around the world. Why are these places so sought after, so longed for, so carefully protected and maintained? More importantly, how can we give our homes these harbor-like elements and provide safe spaces for our families? In the following chapters, we will look into the features that make harbors so welcoming and how to incorporate them into your home.

A harbor is a busy place. Just like your home. It has many elements that must work together for the community to function. In addition to the structure of the place itself, there are the people who live and work there. There are workers, managers, helpers, learners, monitors, supporters, and people in other roles found in a harbor. Mostly, the work and the community function smoothly as all work together and there is peace. In a Harbor Home, there is a place and a role for everyone and practical ways for everyone to contribute to the sanctuary of a harbor home. This book looks at these roles and routines.

Perhaps you are striving to create a Harbor Home for your family but don't really know how to do it. You may feel as though you are drowning in an ocean of chaos and demands and can't even imagine that a safe harbor is within your reach. The purpose of this book is to help you find a way for your home to function as a harbor. You can do this with a few practical, small changes. In this book, we will look at those changes and discuss how your home can become the harbor you are looking for.

Right now, where you are, rest and know that Jesus, the one who calmed the rough seas by speaking to them, is speaking to you. The harbor is near. The harbor is safe. There is a safe space for you and your family in the harbor, and perhaps this book can help your family work together to find it.

Chapter One

THE COVE: A SHELTER IN THE WORLD

I would hurry to my place of shelter, far from the tempest and storm.

Psalm 55:8

The cove at Ocracoke Harbor on the Outer Banks of North Carolina is called Silver Lake and is truly a wonder of a coastline. The water moves gently and there are soft, sandy paths to walk. The sunsets are breathtaking, the restaurants and shops are welcoming, and the entire atmosphere is different from any other place you can visit.

I love Ocracoke Island and go as often as I can. Wandering through the village on foot or a rented bicycle beside the quaint shops feels like a trip to another era. My favorite shop always has a little bucket of bubble solution on the front step along with beautiful bubble wands and an invitation to blow a bubble and make a wish. I always stop to do this. The invitation is simply irresistible.

As I pass the tiny school with a student body of 173 in grades PreK–12, and a student-teacher ratio of 8:1, I imagine what it might be like to attend a school where you are known by all. I imagine teaching in a school where every student is also your neighbor. I wonder if the older students are ever tempted to skip school and if they are, where in the world could they go? Everyone knows everyone else, and it is not a large island. It seems to me that they would get caught pretty easily.

Their school mascot is the Dolphins, but do they have a school song? If so, does everyone in town know the words? These are just a few of the things I wonder about as I wander around. There are other things, but they are even less important than these.

Looking around the village it is obvious that the community has been influenced very little by the outside world. Tourists come by the tens of thousands every year, but still, this community around the cove remains much as it has for decades. The people here set their own standards for how their town functions.

Many of the backroads remain unpaved, some of the signs for businesses are hand-painted. Every shop and restaurant has a bike rack prominently placed in the front of it because cycling is much more popular than driving. Porch swings are everywhere, and the entire town runs at a noticeably slower pace than those bustling towns on the mainland.

Families and friends work together in restaurants and shops, help each other out in times of need, and live harmoniously. Many of the family names that you can see on mailboxes today have been there for generations. Often family homes are occupied by the grandchildren of those who built them. Some of those homes have been converted to retail shops or work areas for artisans who create pottery and woodcrafts and other things to sell. This village is home to many gifted artists and musicians.

Even though people come from all over the world to pick up seashells, buy souvenirs, sit on the beautiful beach and leave their footprints behind, the core of the community is not really changed or deeply impacted. The culture of Ocracoke is carefully kept and protected from too much outside influence.

Silver Lake is a sheltered cove that is the very heart of this harbor. Its presence benefits and defines the entire community. A cove is the central element of any harbor. A cove is a place of shelter which is created by a rounded barrier of land. It is this curved barrier that provides the protection that keeps a cove safe. It is the essential piece that makes the harbor what it is: a community that can be preserved for centuries. Although there are dangers nearby, a cove is a safe place where wind and waves are less likely to be destructive, and the waters are manageable for even the smallest boat.

Looking at a deep, wide cove from the shore, your view of the rough waters beyond is limited. The curve of the land blocks your vision and even though the chaos outside the cove is noticeable, the protected area provides safety and respite from the tempest of the Atlantic. In the cove, everyone feels safe because they are safe. The winds are gentler here. The view is more serene. The water moves but does not destroy.

There are times when you have to leave the cove and go out where you are more vulnerable but, when you do go out into the world beyond, you carry with you the protection that you gain by living your life in the shelter of the cove. And the cove is always waiting for your safe return.

Many adults, especially mothers, feel as though their homes are places of chaos without any real joy and busyness without a clear purpose. Not like the cove of a harbor at all. And there is no wonder why we feel this way. Our lives are full and busy. We often over-schedule ourselves and our family so that when an unexpected event or an emergency happens, we have no room in our schedule to accommodate it. Trying to adjust and redirect our calendars, juggling errands, home repairs, work, school and all the other urgent needs of our families can cause us to feel stressed and inadequate.

We all long for our homes to be a place of refuge from the storms beyond our doors, but we don't always know how to make that happen. Sometimes it may even seem as though the storms are in our homes as often as they are out of them. When there are several anxious, overbooked people in a home conflict is nearly inevitable.

People under stress act out of their frustration and anxiety. This creates an atmosphere in which otherwise kindhearted people who genuinely love each other are simply stretched too thin and tempers flare. Despite all of this, you can have a home in which the level of stress is lowered and the love you have for one another has more freedom to grow.

Here is the central encouraging truth of this book: You can create a Harbor Home. A Harbor Home is one in which the people are connected to one another, everyone has a role that is valued as well as responsibilities that create a sense of belonging. It is a place of unity, peace, and safety.

We can all choose the atmosphere that we want to have within our homes. We cannot have a perfect home, because there is no such thing, but we can have a Harbor Home.

A Harbor Home will be one in which everyone is welcome and everyone has a voice. In a Harbor Home, everyone's talents are noticed and are allowed to be expressed. This is the home that God longs for His children to share and enjoy. We were created to live in families that are bound to one another in love and commitment, solidarity and joy.

A good way to help you to imagine what your Harbor Home can be like is to look at each element of a harbor and then intentionally put those elements in your home. You will be surprised how quickly the smallest changes bring rewards in the form of more peace and joy in your home.

On the pages that follow you will get a lot of fresh ideas for doing the little things and making adjustments that will bring your family together in the harbor that you can create. We will consider each of these elements and how we can use the lessons we learn from a harbor to create the home we all want.

Your Home As a Cove

Let us begin by imagining a cove. A cove is the most noticeable and essential part of any harbor. It is the identifying piece that makes the rest of the harbor possible. The cove is the indispensable part of any harbor, and without it, having a harbor is not realistic.

Coves are not limited to bodies of water, nor are they always natural. Because they are such important spaces, coves have often been created by humans. A cove can be any place of shelter and safety. In fact, you can be instrumental in creating a cove for yourself and your family. We are now going to learn how you can use your body, your countenance, and your words to create a physical, spiritual, and emotional cove in which you and your family can live and love.

A cove in your home is created with small choices, gestures, and changes in outlook made on a consistent basis. These small changes can make large transformations and it doesn't take very long to see results. Some of these changes can create instant positive feedback, so dive right in without overthinking. Virtually everything discussed in this first chapter will be something you can do today with no preparation whatsoever. Do not hesitate to try the things that seem out of your area of comfort. That is where real growth takes place. The Lord is with you.

Let's begin with the only thing we ever can truly control: ourselves. This is the space that is in your jurisdiction and you can use it as a positive influence on others. Your spirit and body are strong and together they can be the foundation of your cove. Focus on your body and the strength it has as you move through the world and your home. Your body is the starting place of the cove of your harbor home. Let us begin.

Your Body As a Cove

Imagine putting your arms up at shoulder level as though you were holding a large beach ball in front of you. With this gesture, you have made a cove of your body. A curved space that shelters and welcomes. Not surprisingly, this is where the cove of your home begins. Once you have decided that you want to create a cove for your family, you begin within your most personal space. The space you alone control.

You did this instinctively the first time your children were placed in your arms. No exhaustion of childbirth or anxiety of waiting for adoption processes to bear fruit stopped you from opening yourself to take in the gift of life that you were being handed. No one had to show you how to create a cove of safety and welcome for your precious little one. You knew how. And you did it.

Once some time passed and the initial shock wore off, you were left with the awesome, overwhelming, long-term task of raising another human being. If you're like most of us, you were scared. You came to understand how vulnerable and completely helpless children really are. You knew that this was going to be the work of a lifetime.

As your children grew you probably also realized that there are not many acts of raising children that are as instinctive as that initial gesture of making a cove of your arms and body. Only the initial act of reaching out for and protecting your child is really instinctive. Everything else, it seems, we have to learn.

Suddenly there are decisions that you have to make and they seem infinite. You have dozens of choices for any given situation. Soccer or karate? Piano or violin? Spank or not? Charter schools, magnet schools, home schools, Christian schools, public schools? How much screen time? Vegetarian? Vegan? Gluten-free? Dairy-free? Free-range kids? Helicopter parenting? The options are dizzying and proponents of each vie for your attention and agreement.

No matter which parenting practices you are comfortable with, you can create a cove that fits. Creating a Harbor Home is not a one size fits all arrangement. Your Harbor Home is uniquely yours no matter who or where you are. A Harbor Home is custom-built.

There is one habit, however, that is a necessity across all parenting practices: It is important to make time to snuggle, hug, cuddle, and hold your children. This is the most effective way to help your child experience the safety of being in the cove of your body. Snuggling is a continuation of the instinctive response we had when our children arrived in our harbor, and we continue this practice for the same reason we began it.

When children are snuggled close all of their senses are engaged. They hear the beat of your heart and the sound of your breathing. They feel the warmth and the weight of your arms surrounding them. They can see the little marks on your skin; the freckles, moles, spots. They smell the special smells that let them know that they are home. Your body can be the safest cove they know.

Children who are often held close have the strength they need to go far. Frequent snuggling offers a security that is unmatched by any other experience. Knowing that you are available gives your children a home base to return to after a time of exploring. Spend time on the floor with your infant and notice how they crawl away from you and then come back. You are the anchor point that lets them have the freedom to wander.

For some people, the act of getting physically close to another body seems awkward or uncomfortable. I understand that there are parents who don't really know how to begin the process of being physically close, so if hugging and snuggling don't come naturally to you, here are some ways to make it more natural in your life and home.

Read Aloud

No matter how old your children are, this is the number one thing to do each day. Early childhood educators can easily spot the children that have the advantage of a parent that reads aloud to them often. Their ability to listen and their reading readiness levels are greater than their peers who do not have this.

Even after my children were teens, we found a time in our crazy busy lives to sit together on the couch while I read to them. I was able to mark the passage of time by the choice of books. *The Cat in the Hat* by Dr. Seuss became *Where the Wild Things Are* by Maurice Sendak.

These were eventually set aside for *Pippi Longstocking* by Astrid Lindgren. Pippi led us to *From The Mixed-Up Files of Mrs. Basil E. Frankweiler* by E.L. Konigsburg and *The Secret Garden* by Frances Burnett. We discovered *The Lion, The Witch, and The Wardrobe* by C.S Lewis and went into Narnia and none of us were ever the same.

When my children grew into adolescence, we read *Anne Frank: The Diary Of A Young Girl* together and were shocked at the depth of inhumanity that people can reach. We cried over *To Kill A Mockingbird* by Harper Lee and were shocked again.

Many times, as my children got older, they'd read aloud to me. We took turns with pages and chapters. These books allowed us to talk about the hard things that exist in the world beyond the safe cove that I was trying to create for them. You will never regret hours spent in this way.

Play a Video Game Together

If you are playing a video game together or taking turns with the same controller, you have a perfect opportunity to cuddle! Set the game for two players and share an ottoman or a similar seating arrangement and sit behind your child.

Wrap your arms around and speak encouraging or enthusiastic words as you engage with the game together. This creates a physical closeness as well as showing an interest in something that interests your child. Additionally, it helps keep the video game from isolating your child from you.

A virtual world can be a solitary world, and in a harbor home, we are a community. When children play games alone in their room for hours on end, they are not getting enough interaction with their family. Make these games something that you do with them.

Let me interject here that I do not enjoy video games in any form. I never have. However, I do now and always have enjoyed my children. To create the cove that they needed to grow into confident adults, I learned to appreciate the opportunities to communicate that video games create.

In addition to all these confessions, let me add that I am terrible at making a video game work properly. That is probably why I never really enjoyed them. Sharing that time and space gave my children an opportunity to be a teacher and I got to be the pupil. It was a nice reversal of roles which gave them a chance to practice leadership skills and for me to model the skills necessary for learning.

When I demonstrated respect for their superior video game skills, they learned to respect my superior long division skills. It was beneficial all the way around. We learned to appreciate each other and the different skills we had to share. It boosted their self-confidence and let me learn how to make a little video creature jump over a canyon.

Play a Board Game Together

Sitting around a table or a space on the floor serves a similar purpose to sitting very close together as in the video game scenario, and for many is more comfortable than being in such close physical contact with another. A board game is a wonderful social activity and gives opportunities to teach good sportsmanship, clear and polite communication skills, and the ability to praise the success of another.

Now, let me make something really, really, really clear at this point. Really clear. The object of playing the game is not to *win* the game, the object of playing the game is to *play* the game. If you are one of those people (and I know you're out there, I'm related to some of you!) who only plays a game to win, then you will be missing the point of this exercise. The object of playing a board game with your child is to (wait for it . . .) play a board game with your child. Play. Sometimes a game is just about playing.

A game is simply a vehicle to communicate with your child, encourage your child, and build a cove. If you or your child gets angry about the game or accuses another player of "cheating" or reacts with excessive negativity when you roll a four but need a six, you really should work on that. In fact, you absolutely should work on that.

A game is for play, so play nicely. Enjoy the people you are with. Laugh. Play. Talk. That's what you do in a harbor home. In our cove, we often make time for play, and everyone plays nicely.

Until you are comfortable with being close, these are some great techniques to get you there. If you are someone who is comfortable being close, these techniques will be very easy for you, and you can include them as you continue to create a cove.

Your Countenance As a Cove

Your countenance is how your face and body communicate. It communicates to those around you when you are not speaking. There have been a great many scientific studies about non-verbal communication, and most of them reveal that 90 percent or more of all communication is non-verbal.

Think about the cashier at the store who is ready to go home for the day. He or she doesn't have to tell you this; you know it by their countenance. It is written on the face or in the drooping of the shoulders. They are communicating without speaking. Their countenance reveals all. Your countenance reveals a good deal about you, too.

With an open, positive countenance it is possible for you to alter the stress level in you and around you. It is helpful to practice the countenance that creates a cove even when you don't "feel like it". Take it one step further: practice doing this *especially* when you don't "feel like it". Practice this often until it becomes a natural habit. Behavior experts assure us that anything you consistently do becomes a habit that you do without having to work at it. Take the time to do this.

Check in with your own countenance right now. Is it welcoming? Would you seem approachable to a tired child, an anxious teen, or a stressed adult? Is gravity dictating your countenance by pulling your mouth down into a frown? Be honest with yourself. Look in a mirror and check. Now, let's try an exercise.

Practice Smiling

Right now, where you are, smile. Just smile. Hold it for a moment. Practice this. Smile again. Hold it a little longer than the last time. Read a few more sentences then check in again. If the smile has gone, smile again.

A smile is the beginning of creating a cove for your family and yourself. It is a voluntary motion and is the baseline of your countenance. A smile is even shaped like a cove! It is the universal language of peace and kindness.

In addition, your smile is contagious. It is nearly impossible to resist smiling back at someone who is smiling at you. Think about a time when someone smiled a genuine smile at you. Just the memory of it brings a smile to your face. Think about a time when the pleasure of seeing someone you love brought a smile so big you didn't think your face could contain it. Keep that memory. And smile.

Pass the smile along to the people in your cove. Check in with your countenance. Are you smiling? If not, go ahead and do it. Create a cove with the expression on your face. Look in a mirror. Practice different smiles until you find the one you like most.

Imagine that right now God is looking at you the way you looked at your newborn baby. Experience love and peace, and then share it. Practice this smile. A warm and open countenance typically contains a smile that is relaxed and calm. With practice, this kind of smile can be achieved easily and naturally. And yes, I did use the word "practice" in association with smiling.

When you are creating a cove with your countenance, the most helpful habit you can cultivate is the habit of smiling. It is well worth developing. Smiling is a simple way to create a cove for yourself as well as for others. Besides all this, smiling is actually good for you! Your brain doesn't know if you are faking a smile or not, so when you smile, your mind responds with calm and happiness even if your life is not calm and happy.

Don't reserve your smiles for when everything is going well. Those moments are rare. If you are feeling pushed and stressed and overwhelmed, check in with your countenance and smile. This habit reduces stress, boosts your immune system, and releases endorphins. And it is free.

The Eyes Have It

Your countenance is about more than smiling. Your countenance contains all the communication you are sending out without speaking. Your eyes communicate particularly well. Are your eyes focused on the one with whom you are communicating, or are they roving the room? Looking directly at someone with whom you are speaking offers the intimate connection that happens in a cove.

Maintain steady, calm eye contact whenever you are dealing with those who are close to you. Be especially careful to practice this with children. Children will speak openly to those who listen openly. If a child is speaking to you, turn your eyes to them.

Arms, Shoulders, Knees, and Toes

The way you hold your arms and the direction in which you point your feet are a part of your countenance in addition to the control you exercise over your eyes. Notice how you stand when you are communicating. With an open countenance, your shoulders are loose and parallel to the ground. You are standing up straight and relaxed. Resist the urge to fold your arms in front of your body when you are communicating with others. This signals that you are closed to anything that may be said to you. You send the message that you are excluding those around you.

If you feel awkward and don't know what to do with your hands, hold them in front of you with relaxed arms and shoulders. and smile. Notice also where your feet are pointing as you are speaking or listening to someone. If your feet are pointing toward the one with whom you are speaking, you are sending the message of careful attention and full engagement. When you are engaged in conversation with anyone, make a point of turning so that your toes are pointing toward them and that the rest of your body does too.

The posture that communicates that you are functioning as a cove is comfortable and upright. Slouching communicates defeat, and Harbor Homes are never defeated! Stand up straight as you walk, and walk with purpose.

When you combine these features of your countenance, you will not only appear more confident and welcoming, you will feel it as well. An open posture communicates to others and to yourself that you are focused on the present and not fretting about what has gone before or that which is yet to come.

Similar to the way that smiling sends messages of wellbeing to your brain, an open and confident posture fools the brain into believing that you are comfortable and confident even when you are not. Because of this, you are creating a cove not only for those around you but for yourself as well.

The safety of the cove is for you as well as for those you love. Welcome yourself to the cove with your countenance. Your countenance is a vital part of creating a cove in your harbor home. The cove, as you remember, is the central element of a harbor, and your countenance is the central element of creating a cove in your harbor home. Practice these habits and let them be a blessing to everyone! Including you.

Your Heart As a Cove

It is said that children spell love T-I-M-E. This truth is carried across all strong relationships. We give our time to the people and activities that are the most important to us. In essence, when we give our time to our families we are actually giving our heart.

When we give someone time, we are giving something that is more valuable than anything else we possess because we cannot manufacture more of it. We can earn more money, make more gifts, imagine more experiences, but we only have the time we have been appointed. Giving it freely to another is to share the essence of life.

In a cove, time is spent as positively as possible. Disputes are handled quickly and produce an outcome that keeps relationships intact. Time is too precious to waste it being unkind or impatient. When your heart is a cove, you choose to involve yourself in an uplifting way with those who share your space. Give your heart by giving positive time to those in your cove.

So often, I've heard people say that they "don't have time" to sit down and play or read with their children and other loved ones. Let me say very clearly that you can make time for anything that truly matters. Strictly limit isolated screen time for everyone in the family. Turn off the television. Stop texting. Get off of Facebook, Instagram, Tik Tok, YouTube, Pinterest, Candy Crush, or whatever draws you to pick up your phone every three minutes. Focus on the ones you love without frequent distractions.

Simply live in the cove and be present in the lives of those around you. You can do it. Remember that there will come a day when the only laundry in the hamper will be yours, the only meals you will prepare will be for yourself, the only noise in the house will come from you. You can use the time you have with your family all together any way you choose. Choose to make a cove of your heart.

Here is a reminder of the truth: once you are alone in your home you probably won't look back and wish you had watched more television. You'll wish for more games of Candyland and more kites flown on breezy Saturday mornings. Trips to big-box theme parks will not be more meaningful or create better memories than making up new words to old songs as you ride in the car. Use your moments well. Moments are how you spend your life. This is your cove, and you can cherish it.

Your Words As a Cove

When my children were small I taught them a modified version of an old proverb. It went this way: *Sticks and stones will break my bones but words will break my heart.* I used it as a reminder and a mantra that I expected the words that we spoke to one another to be uplifting or, at least, not harmful. I reminded them that words are powerful and easily cause wounds that are not easily healed. In our cove, we were to be cautious with our words.

Were we always cautious with our words? Of course not. But we learned how to quickly and sincerely say "I'm sorry" when we were unkind. Apologies were quick to be spoken and forgiveness quickly given.

One of the most important truths concerning words is that once they have been spoken, they cannot ever be unspoken. They are like arrows shot from a bow. They are flung out from our mouths into the minds of those who hear them, and there they rest.

Sometimes our words rest and reverberate in the minds of others for decades. Kind words or hurtful words, they linger on. Choose your words carefully so that they will strengthen and sustain your cove. Remind your children that in your cove, words are used to build each other up and not tear each other down.

Our words can influence healing or pain, courage or fear, hope or despair. There is no way to overstate the power of the spoken word. Surely you can pause and remember clearly the words of someone who spoke to you and those words gave you the desire to accomplish something great or try something new. Someone told you that you were strong or smart or creative and you were inspired to use your gifts.

Perhaps you can also remember someone who said something to you and those words influenced you to give up on a dream or to think of yourself as unattractive or unworthy. The writer of the book of Proverbs has a lot to say about this. My favorite is this: *Gracious words are a honeycomb, sweet to the soul and healing to the bones* (Proverbs 16:24).

It is clear that the words of those we are close to can either heal or harm, so it is very important that the words spoken in your harbor home always come from a place of love and peace. There are many techniques for keeping your words truthful and loving. Words matter, so make sure that your words are good and true.

Here are some ways to get better at controlling your words instead of allowing your words to go unchecked.

Stop

One time-honored way of getting control over your angry or hurtful words is to simply count several numbers before speaking. In other words, pause. Stop. Don't speak until you've gotten beyond the initial reaction. Just. Don't. Speak. Wait until you know that you won't later regret what you're going to say.

It is a bad feeling to be surprised by the words coming out of your own mouth! Trust me on this one. It's a bad feeling. As the Apostle Paul assured us, *Instead, speaking the truth in love we will become in every respect the mature body of him who is the head, that is, Christ* (Ephesians 4:15).

Practice

Another way is to practice (there's that word again . . .) what you want to say before a situation occurs. Have you noticed how often you find yourself in the same situations or conversations with your children, spouse, or other members of your family? In family dynamics, a lot of little scenes are replayed often. It's like déjà vu all over again, as Yogi Berra said. Same conflict, same conversations. Different day.

I find it helpful to keep a mental list and, on occasion, a written list of the best, most positive responses I can make in the situations or conversations that are replayed over and over in our harbor home.

Go ahead and stop right now and make a note, written or mental, about the scenarios in your harbor home that are replayed over and over. Some are funny, some are neutral, but some bring negative words and responses virtually every time. You dread these recurring interactions, you see them on the horizon, and yet you are usually unprepared to respond in a manner that represents the cove that we are creating in our Harbor Home.

Imagine a positive response to the situations that drain away peace instead of replenishing it. Begin now to realize that you can choose a response that will build the cove you want in the harbor. Like the other habits in this chapter, this one takes practice. Look at a few examples of responses that reflect life in a cove:

Positively State the Expectation

When you are expressing what you expect the children around you to be doing (or not doing) a helpful technique is to express that expectation in positive terms. Let me explain what I mean.

Imagine this scenario: your nine-year-old comes in from school and drops his book bag on the floor of the laundry room. You want it to be taken to the hook by the front door so that it can be ready for the next morning.

Rather than raising your voice, berating him, and telling him that you have told him a million times that his book bag does not go on the floor (even though you have) remind him calmly and firmly what he should do with his book bag. Your words could be similar to this: "Your book bag goes on the hook by the door. You know this. Take it there now please." Or you can say, "You know where the book bag goes."

It is important to note that your voice is calm, your eyes are on the same level as his eyes, your feet are pointing at him and you are using a low tone of voice. A firm, loving tone eliminates the need for raised, harsh voices. This technique makes very clear the behavior you do want, as opposed to focusing on behavior you do not want. Positively state the expectation. Express what you want, not what you don't want. Stay calm while doing so.

Refrain From Using Upspeak

Upspeak, or rising intonation, is very common among Americans. This is the habit many of us have of speaking our phrases with a higher tone at the end of them. This effectively turns statements into questions. The implication is that you are offering a choice.

Unless you truly are offering a choice, your inflection should remain flat. Look at this example: the entire family is leaving for baseball practice in forty-five minutes, and you must all eat dinner before you go. The meal is prepared and ready to serve, but your nine-year-old is lingering at his tablet. So you say, "Sweetie, put your tablet down and come eat . . . okay?" Or "Honey, can you come on now, please?" He doesn't budge.

Instead of these ineffective, wheedling phrases, try clearly and positively speaking your expectation with no upspeak or ending the statement with "Okay?" Asking "Okay?" is another way of implying that a choice is available. So try phrasing it this way. "Dinner is ready now. Put down your tablet, wash your hands and come to the table please."

In a harbor home, there are times when individuals may choose their activities, and times when the greater good of the family must be respected and therefore all must cooperate with the schedule. When cooperation is needed, cooperation must be expected. State the expectation.

Remember to keep your tone low, your inflection flat and your words firm and calm. If you have to repeat the directions, remind the child that the tablet could be forfeited the next day as a reminder of the expectations in a harbor home.

Verbalize Only Consequences You Are Willing to Pursue

We all reach a point at which we feel completely at our wit's end and as though we've used all our positive options. At such a time it is tempting to issue dire threats that you know in your heart you will never follow through on. Doing this completely erodes your credibility and demonstrates that you are no longer in control of the harbor home.

Let me be very clear about this: your children want you to be in control of the harbor in which they live. They know that without you in control they are not safe. Often, out-of-bounds behavior is simply a way to make sure that you are still in control.

Families in which the adults are loving, firm, and clearly in charge produce children who are secure and ready to take their place in the world. They learn how to create their own harbor when the time comes. So unless you are actually going to use a bungee cord to secure your child to the roof rack of your car and drive them to the closest orphanage, don't tell them that you're going to do that. Just a suggestion.

Bribery Is Counterproductive

Bribery may seem like a good idea in a trying moment but, in the long run, offering a tangible reward for reasonable and cooperative behavior backfires. Remember that in a Harbor Home we work together because we are a community that loves and depends on another. Being part of a family that shares responsibilities and works well to help each other is worth more in the long run than any five-dollar trinket you can offer. So maybe don't promise a new soccer ball if the child will just brush their teeth before leaving to go to school. Or whatever.

The one who is expected to cooperate with the community today will certainly need to rely on the community's cooperation later. Life in a Harbor Home is a series of sacrifices and generosity. Giving and receiving are necessary for all to be safe and loved.

Model Encouragement

The people around you are listening to and absorbing your words. As an adult in the leadership of your harbor home, your example of encouraging those who live in the harbor with you is vital. Look for and find reasons to offer encouragement and praise.

When encouragement is the most common conversation heard, the times when you must speak out in correction will be distinct, and therefore more likely to be heard. If your words are more often corrective and discouraging, they are more likely to be dismissed when you really need them to be heard. Make your encouragement frequent and lavish. Keep your corrections rare and succinct.

Bad Words

When I say "bad words" you know the words I mean. Profanity has no place in your . . . well, it has no place anywhere. If you are reading this book, I assume you are out of middle school and, therefore, beyond the need to show off your extensive vocabulary of foul language. We are called to walk on a higher road in all areas of life.

Remember that words can't be unsaid, and there are so many alternatives to these profane and meaningless words. Train yourself to use language that uplifts and if these words are in your daily conversation pattern, stop. Your children are listening and will repeat every phrase you use. Every phrase. At the worst possible moment. Words matter. Use words that are in good taste and bring honor to your home.

Your Home As a Cove

When your family is at home, where is everybody? Is someone in the kitchen, someone else in the office, one child is in the den, and the other is somewhere and being suspiciously quiet?

Certainly, there are times almost every day when your family will be scattered throughout your house even if you are in a small house like mine, a tiny apartment like my daughter's, or a large house like some of my neighbors'. In a harbor home, however, there should come a time each day when the family purposefully comes together to be in a shared space. If your family doesn't have this habit yet, you can begin it today.

When you are in this shared space, acknowledge each other. Speak. Say hi. Express pleasure at being together with your family. When I was a young mother with my first baby daughter in my arms I decided that every time I saw her I would tell her that I was glad to see her. Every time. Every day. And so I did. I still do this four decades later, and I believe that it has helped us to remain close all this time.

My son and his wife, like many parents, have a daily practice of asking the twins during dinner "What was the best thing that happened today?" They all take turns, and everybody gets a chance to speak uninterrupted. It is a beautiful moment that is part of each day in their very busy harbor home.

After this exchange, it's more than okay to watch a movie or do independent activities. But remember: family together time is not the time to criticize a sloppily made bed or unkempt hair. This should be a positive time when you are simply in your cove and all is well. Praise the accomplishments. Compliment the outfit. Notice the good things.

Share the space, look at each other. Smile at your spouse and your children. Let them catch you giving them a loving glance or looking at them with admiration. If you love them and you know it, your face will surely show it!

Life in the cove of your harbor will have days that are good and days that serve as teaching moments. Using these tools you can create a cove that offers shelter from the storms beyond and provides a place of safety for you and for everyone around you.

Summary of Chapter One

Creating a cove is a one day at a time, one step at a time project. Chances are very high that you are already halfway there and are doing much better than you realize. Don't push yourself to implement all of these strategies in one day or even all of them every day. If you have picked up this book you probably already have more ideas and methods than these. Give yourself credit for all you are already doing. Make a list of all the things that you do well in your harbor home and read them when you feel discouraged.

Your love for your family is the most important element for creating the cove of your harbor home. Your love is unique and cannot be offered to your family by anyone else. You are doing that already, so stand encouraged. You are on the right road. You don't have to be perfect. God created you to be good, not perfect.

Remember from the first chapter of Genesis that when God created the world He said that it was good. Nowhere in the entire creation story did God declare that anything was perfect. We are all good in God's eyes. We don't always do good things, but we are good because we were created by God. Every one of us. You are good. I am good. I feel a little better now, do you? Sometimes we all need that reminder. Remind yourself that you are good.

You need a harbor home too. A cove, as I mentioned at the beginning of this chapter, is a curved shelter. The curve of the land that creates this shelter provides a barrier between that which is within it and the chaos that lies beyond it. Understand this about the cove of a harbor home: it is for you as well. I repeat: the cove is for you. You have a responsibility for contributing to creating it and for teaching those around you to contribute as well, but, the cove is for you to experience safety and peace and then to share it together. Be sheltered. Be loved.

Questions for Discussion or Deeper Thinking

1. If someone created a harbor home for you when you were growing up, what is your happiest memory?
2. What parts of creating a cove for your family are you already doing? Describe in detail.
3. What new element do you want to add to your cove? What will you have to change to add this?

4. Do you have a space in your home in which everyone can be together in a comfortable way? What is it about this space that makes it welcoming?
5. How do you encourage kindness in your Harbor Home?

Chapter Two

THE DEEP WATER: THE FAITH THAT HOLDS US

I would hurry to my place of shelter far from the tempest and storm.

Psalm 55:8

A key element of a safe harbor is that the water is deep. Deep water is important to mariners. Every wise captain, no matter how large or small their vessel, knows exactly how much of their craft is below the waterline, and they always ensure that the vulnerable underside of their boat is well above the seafloor.

Experienced boaters know that the floor of any body of water is strewn with rocks and debris and is made of hills and valleys similar to those on land. Unlike the hills and valleys on land, those that are under the water can change quite quickly. So when the water is deep, the concern of running aground and having their vessel destroyed is far from their minds.

Proficient watermen are constantly monitoring the environment under the water's surface, particularly the water directly beneath their boats. They study charts. Charts contain information about the water similar to what maps contain about roads on land. Boaters listen carefully to weather bulletins. They scan the water's surface for signs of change which could indicate a change below the surface. They pay close attention to radioed "Warnings To Mariners" coming from different agencies such as the Coast Guard or the National Weather Service. They communicate with other captains and watch the electronic devices on their boats. They are aware and alert at all times.

This is particularly true in a setting such as the coast of North Carolina where the water is turbulent and powerful. Experienced boaters are continually on watch. Last week's weather bulletin is not good enough if they must enter the shipping lanes today. They constantly study and scan their surroundings to make sure that they are on course and that the water below their vessel is deep enough.

To all seafarers, a deep water harbor is especially prized. Captains and crew need rest from the constant concern and vigilance that is necessary for the open water. In the harbor, captains find peace and a chance to catch their breath. Captains moor their boats in the harbor, enjoy some respite, and get some much-needed rest. When they are in a deep water harbor, they know they and their crew are safe, and that the boat remains steady.

During a tsunami such as the one that devastated Thailand in 2004, ships are only safe in the deep water far off the shore.

It is the shallow coastal areas that create the destructive walls of water that kill all living things in its path. That tsunami, born of an earthquake some distance away, brought near-total destruction to Thailand's coast. The unimaginable waves swept away those who were onshore or in the shallows that day, and the result was catastrophic devastation. The boats and people who survived and were not injured were the ones who were far away from the shore in the very deep water.

In a Harbor Home, it is faith that provides the deep, still waters in which we can safely moor our families. It is faith, when it is deep and strong beneath us, that keeps us buoyed up and confident that we are cared for by an eternal love. Faith is a great gift that you can develop in your Harbor Home, and this chapter is dedicated to helping you to learn how to develop faith within yourself and how to share that with your family.

We will be looking into some concrete things that you can do that will lead you and your family to hear and experience God, but also concepts that you can consider or reconsider as your faith grows.

Faith Communities

The deep-water kind of faith that we carry through our lives gives us common ground with those faithful ones who have gone before us, the faithful yet to be born, and the believers with whom we share our community. We are included in a rich heritage that has been an integral part of civilization for centuries.

Through our faith, we are each a link in a strong and mighty chain. Being attached to a faithful, God-centered community church congregation adds depth to your faith and helps you maintain the deep water in the harbor you call home.

People of faith often question the need for being part of a larger group of believers. There are several reasons for this. One is that weekly attendance is challenging and cuts into private family time. Another is that many of us have a sense of mistrust toward a church that looks like an institution.

People who have left their faith communities cite having been hurt or witnessing unkind behavior as one of the reasons they no longer want to participate. Sadly, this happens far too often in faith communities. Others say that a faith community doesn't meet their needs or has nothing real to offer their family. All these observations have a certain validity. However, there are powerful reasons to take a fresh look at them:

1. While a person can worship in private, it is nearly impossible to truly grow in knowledge or understanding without being able to share ideas with people in a faith community who have different faith experiences than your own.
2. A true disciple of any faith is disciplined in that faith. Disciple and discipline are almost the same words. The truly faithful among us are committed to reading, learning, and maturing their faith. This is much more likely to happen in a community of believers.
3. Children are helped and encouraged in their faith when they see and hear it coming from other respected and loving adults in their community. Children are great observers of behavior and when they see many adults echoing your

family beliefs those practices take root more easily in their hearts and minds. A loving teacher at church can be a friend that your child will remember all their life.

4. Setting aside one or two hours a week to attend worship services is a healthy practice for humans. We are spiritual beings in human bodies. Nurturing the spirit is an important part of our humanity.
5. The very core of Christianity is community. The gospels teach us that Christ lived in community, not in an isolated monastery. Christians who neglect this aspect of the faith are missing a vital piece of Christ's message. We were never meant to keep our faith private or hide ourselves away from other believers. We are called to bear witness to the truth of Christ and, therefore, are better when we gather together routinely.

Well-cultivated faith becomes a richer experience when it is shared with those in your home. In addition, faith matures better and more easily when you are connected with a community of believers. Proverbs 27:17 expresses this beautifully when it says, *As iron sharpens iron, so one person sharpens another.*

As theologians across the centuries have observed, a Christian worshiping alone is like an ember taken out of the fire; it cools very quickly. God designed us for community living and wants us to live together peacefully while urging each other to be better.

Strengthening Your Children and Their Faith

Helping your children and adolescents to develop a faith that they can call their own is a crucial part of Christian parenting.

Your children are more likely to enjoy nurturing their faith if they are surrounded by adults who encourage them and friends that are making the journey with them. When children and adolescents have friends their own age who share their faith, it helps them to maintain it for their lifetime. However, in helping your child develop their faith, there is no substitute for your input in some simple and practical ways.

Prayer and Worship At Home

Keep the Organic Conversations Going

When my children were young there was a very big emphasis on "family devotion time" in Christian homes. There were a lot of books and other resources available for this and the technique most often suggested was to read a devotion guide and a passage of Scripture each day after dinner or before breakfast or at some prescribed time of the day.

There was only one problem. Most of these resources were mind-numbingly dull, sanctimonious in their tone and I did not think that they were written by people who understood children very well. At least not my children. A lot of moms I knew reported the same issue.

So I tried another technique and, frankly, at the time, I did not think that I was really "doing it right" when it came to devotion time for my children. I was really hard on myself about raising my children in a Christian home. Since I was not raised that way and I didn't have a strong example of how to do it, I read and listened to everything on the topic that I could find and tried to follow through on all of it. My poor kids!

Eventually, I realized that what really worked was to simply keep organic conversations going. By organic conversations I mean that our faith was a topic that came up often and naturally as time went on. I very seldom sat the children down and insisted that we "talk about religious things." The topic came up organically as we observed our world and moved through our days.

Organic conversations begin where you are. When my children and I were working on math problems I would casually mention that only God could be in charge of something as simple as 2+2 and at the same time the complexities of the Pythagorean theorem and have all of it be exact and perfect every single time.

Mathematical studies are remarkable in that they are universal and cut through all cultures. Math reminds me of when God called Himself "I Am." Or, more literally, "I am being that which I am being" because math is what it is. No opinions or arguments can change the math. Neither can God be changed by our opinions.

In addition to organic conversations, keep reading or telling age-appropriate stories about great Christian leaders. Also, set a strong example of living as close to a Christ-like life as you can. Read Scripture in small portions and ask good questions about what is read. Refer to Jesus in your conversations. Model the love of Christ in your words and actions.

Be Jesus in This Moment

Ask your children what they think Jesus would have us do in whatever situation you are in. Are you waiting in a long line at the grocery store? Talk about how Jesus wants us to be patient and kind. Smile at the others who are also waiting in line. Strike up a conversation with the people around you. Be kind and friendly.

Are you driving all the way to grandma's house? Spend some of the time singing songs about Jesus. Ask questions about what the song means. Can you make up a new verse that adds to the song? Jesus would have been taught songs when He was a child. The songs of His faith are found in the book of Psalms in our Bible. Singing our faith is a joy-filled way to put our faith in our hearts and minds.

Talk about Jesus and the world in which He lived in an open, unforced, familiar way throughout each day. Begin even more organic conversations. Tell or read about great Biblical heroes. Point out that those people were people very much like us with parents, siblings, friends, and flaws. Tell what you know, then go learn more and tell about that. Be the teacher filled with wonder; the disciple filled with joy. It is contagious.

See God in Everything

In this, we are continuing to use organic conversations. Use the world itself to communicate the love of God to your children. When you see a rainbow in the sky, talk about how the sun passing through the water droplets in the air separates the light into all those colors and they are projected on the clouds like a movie screen.

But then, tell them about the very first people that God showed a rainbow to. Talk about Noah and how he was commanded by God to save the animals of earth from the great flood and when the flood was over, God put the rainbow in the sky as the sign of His promise that never again would the earth be destroyed with water. The rainbow is still a sign of God's great love, and a wonderful science lesson to boot!

Flowers blooming in the spring, leaves turning colors in the fall, snow in the winter, a fire burning in your firepit, ocean waves, sand on the beach. All these things are created by God and are there for you and your children to explore! Explore not just the creation and the creator, but also the science that people have discovered. God is everywhere we are. All you have to do is point it out to your children. Talk about God as naturally as you talk about anything else and find Him in the nature of the world.

End Each Day Well

Praying with your children before going to sleep at night is a beautiful, simple practice that you can begin on the very first night that they are born. Spend a moment resting your hand on your child and pray aloud. As they get older, invite them to pray aloud also. This custom ends each day well and reminds them that as they sleep God is still with them. In a home filled with Christ's love, there is a strong emphasis on peace and love. Ending each day with calm, reassuring, quiet prayer goes a long way to counteracting the confusion, conflict, and chaos of the day.

Your Children and Faith Communities

Just like adult Christians, young Christians are more likely to develop a deep faith when they are an active part of a faith community. Regularly attending worship and programs geared for their age group will help your children to make friends among the other children that are there. The key is to regularly attend. When your children attend sporadically or only when they "feel like it" or when you don't have any other plans, they will feel less comfortable than they would if they were at each gathering.

Get Them to Youth Group Each Week

If you find that your children say that the group is "boring" or "no fun" or "they don't have friends there," I urge you to have them go anyway. Check into what is going on in their group. Chances are there are games and fellowship, snacks and adults who care about kids. This is a great start. Give your kids time to get comfortable with the group.

If the church where you worship doesn't have a youth ministry program or your child's friends go to another youth program, let them go with their friends. This will help them enjoy it, make more friends, and put them all in an atmosphere where they are likely to have an encounter with Jesus. Even if your family has attended the same church since the Mayflower landed in Massachusetts, if it doesn't have a youth group, take your child to a program that helps them grow and enjoy friends.

Your children's youth group probably won't offer the same kind of fun that is offered at an amusement park or an arcade or other commercial entertainment venue, and it isn't supposed to. Youth group is not Disney World. Amusement parks are not about relationship building; youth groups are. Before you allow your child to skip youth fellowship, because it is "boring", consider that your goal is to set them up to make faithful friends and urge them to go and have a good time.

Let's just get really real here about tweenagers and teenagers. They may tell you that it is boring at their youth group and they don't want to go but, trust me on this one. They are almost certainly having fun once they get there. Seriously. The kids who get in your car after youth and say that they "didn't do anything" have probably been playing volleyball or been in some kind of crazy relay race involving shaving cream. They have also laughed at dumb jokes, had some kind of snack, and been taught an easily digestible lesson about Christ and how to be a more faithful follower. They are having more fun than they are willing to say, and they want you to encourage them to go back. Really.

Mission Trips

A very popular way for Christian teenagers to live out their faith is to go on mission trips. This is, in general, a wonderful thing. The idea of traveling to a place where the people are less privileged is very appealing. Packing duffle bags with paintbrushes, hammers, and matching t-shirts is exciting, the trip is a great adventure, and traveling to a new environment is a great educational opportunity.

Obviously, there are a lot of factors involved in considering whether or not your child should go on one of these trips and there are a lot of potential pitfalls to them. Use your best judgment and check into all the details. For example: How many adults are going? How committed are they to making sure that every child is where they are supposed to be at any given time? Is there a behavior covenant or a dress code? If not, there should be. Ask lots of questions before you pay for a mission trip.

As a rule, I prefer for mission work to remain local. I know that many faithful people are called to lands far away and that those efforts are often blessed and used by God. But Jesus told us to love our neighbors. When I hear these words it encourages me to believe that we should begin with our actual neighbors. This is not a scriptural statement, but a personal preference after years of doing both long-distance and local missions with youth.

First of all, long-distance mission trips are expensive and, for the Christian educator planning these trips, it is very hard to include everyone. Fundraising often only goes so far.

Second of all, teens don't necessarily know how to handle themselves in another culture and may either act out inappropriately or cling very close to a trusted adult. I've seen both happen. Remember this: mission trips are a lot of hard work that is often physical work. These trips are tiring and put teenagers in close contact with one another for several days with no break.

This is not meant to discourage you from sending your children on mission trips, but rather to encourage you to know all the dynamics, ask a lot of questions and pray beforehand. I have seen these trips transform teenagers into fervent believers and followers of Christ. Pray and find out details upfront.

Another reason I like for missions to remain local is due to an experience I had while serving a church in a neighborhood that had changed dramatically in the twenty or thirty years or so before my arrival.

The community had, until that point, been mostly made up of small rural farms and suburban homes on large lots. It had, around the time of the late 1960s and into the 1970s, transitioned to a lower-income neighborhood in our suburb of the city. The older original residents had mostly moved away to other areas but continued to attend the church even though the drive was up to forty minutes. They longed for the old days.

Like many neighborhoods similar to this one there was a large population of elderly people who needed help maintaining their homes and having things done like getting ramps installed to their doors or smoke detectors replaced. Little projects like these are very often beyond the capability of people who are older or infirm.

It seemed to me that we could love our neighbors that were actually, well, our neighbors. I thought it was a great idea to love the ones who lived in our backyard by serving them as we would serve those who live hundreds of miles away. It made sense to me. But, not everyone agreed with me. In fact, almost no one agreed with me.

I suggested this radical idea at a meeting of the people that made the decisions about where and how to spend money designated for the missions of the church. I told them that my reasoning was that this project was less expensive than traveling to a similar situation several states away and was at the same time loving our neighbors.

It only took a few moments for the objections to begin. With varying degrees of hostility, I was told that not one dime of our mission money would be spent on such a project. I was then regaled, for the umpteenth time, with tales of how glorious that neighborhood had once been. What a perfect place to live it once was. And now it was . . . not. The older ones who felt displaced by the changes to the community had their say and they got their way. We did not do any mission work for our neighbors.

Fast forward two summers. I was in the part of the churchyard which ran along the edge of the sidewalk of this neighborhood and saw a group of teens in matching t-shirts walking along looking around with a couple of adult leaders. I recognized them to be a youth group, and since I didn't know them, I approached to introduce myself and offer a welcome to them.

It turned out that they were a youth group from about 350 miles away who had come to do mission work in our neighborhood.

The week-long trip was to include, I was told, building two ramps, repairing a few roofs, doing several lawn care projects, and smoke detector checks for anyone who wanted it.

I praised them for their dedication and hard work and expressed welcome and asked if they needed anything. I thanked them for being the hands and feet of Jesus in our neighborhood. They thanked me, said that they were well supplied, and then continued their tour.

I went inside and into my office and shut the door. I wanted to cry my tears of shame in private. As much as I understood the anxiety our older members felt at feeling that they no longer fit in the community where they raised their children, I also recognized that each and every one of them had moved to lovely, comfortable homes in lovely, comfortable neighborhoods. They could have made a very different decision. My face was burning with shame.

I was so disappointed in the way that our membership had responded to the proposal that we minister to our neighbors. I was so disappointed in myself that I hadn't raised money and gathered people on my own and organized a mission that was not associated with our church.

It took a while for me to move past the feeling that I had failed to be Jesus in our neighborhood. I learned a lot from that experience. From that day to this I have been passionate about working for the Lord where we live.

Authenticity

Young people have a remarkable radar for faith practices that either fail to support or completely deny the faith that they have heard professed. If your children are going to accept the faith that you have been teaching them they must see that it is real. It must be authentic. It must be lived out in practical and meaningful ways. Mission opportunities in which the entire family can participate can be a real demonstration of the love of Christ. This can also help your children see how you and other Christians live what they believe. Consider allowing your child to participate, and consider serving beside them.

Authentic Christian faith manifests itself in kind and respectful behavior toward all people no matter their race, nationality, or any other group designation. Authentic Christian faith does not have a political agenda that identifies with one party over another. Authentic Christians worship freely and support the leadership of their church, the community, and the secular government. If your faith practices are tied closely to your politics or if you fail to live your faith then you run a great risk of your child rejecting your faith.

Your children will eventually make a choice about their faith. You can be a strong and loving influence on that choice and help them by giving them as many opportunities as possible to encounter Jesus. This will not guarantee that they will remain faithful into their adult years because, as with the rest of humankind, your children were given free will by God. Your best tool is prayer. Consistent, fervent, faithful.

Offer them love and support, information, and opportunities. Listen to them. Respond with respect and honesty. Churches are flawed like every community. If your church has issues, talk openly about them. Help your child to see the best in others and also see how they can be their best as they learn and grow. Help them find ways to serve in your own congregation.

They, like you, are going to make many mistakes and poor decisions as they move through the adolescent years. They may question your faith. They may reject your faith. This is normal as they work out what it means to be independent adults. Remain calm and steady. Keep on being Jesus in their lives and in the lives of others. As Saint Francis of Assisi said, "Preach the gospel at all times. When necessary, use words."

Your job is to teach your children with strength and grace. Strength and grace are the twin children of any faithful heart. They are like gears in a fine watch; both are necessary for faith to be passed along. Neither of these two attributes can be successfully faked. Strength and grace. They are either genuine or they are not there at all.

Your children are experts on you. They will always know the difference between a faith that is genuine and one that is counterfeit. Young people are more likely to embrace your faith when they see it lived out in you with authenticity, sincerity, and consistency. Pray for these things.

Strengthening the Faith Inside Your Own Heart

Faith that sustains a Harbor Home requires private attention. It is in the moments that you spend alone with God that you get close to Him and He to you. The real work of drawing near to God is done privately and even secretly. Jesus encourages us in Matthew 6:6 to go and spend time alone with God in private. Doing so has benefits that are not obvious at first glance. Here are just a few:

- **Intimacy:** In privacy with God there is intimacy. You have no distractions and nothing that is between you and God.

In a time and space of privacy, you can focus clearly on listening to His voice. You are one of His sheep, and you recognize His voice as your Shepherd. He calls out to your heart and you can hear Him because you are alone with Him. This level of intimacy with God is unique to these moments of privacy. Once you have begun to develop this closeness with the Lord in private moments, you will begin to crave that time when you and God are alone together.

- **Honesty:** When you are alone with the Lord there is no way to pretend that you are anything other than who and what you are. There is no one that you have to pretend to be strong for, no one to impress with your beautiful prayers, no one to see that you are feeling lost and afraid, and no one who is watching you cover all that with arrogance. You and God alone know who you are at the innermost part of you, and God loves you at that deepest place. Without the time spent with Him in secret, you may never be able to openly express those things that you and God both know. And then you will never know the amount of love and grace He has poured into you. Just be honest with God and yourself. Go whisper your secrets. It is okay.
- **Purposefulness:** To have these private moments alone with God, we have to make it happen on purpose. If you have a family with young children it is very challenging to get a moment to yourself. A lot of mothers report that they don't even get to go to the bathroom alone. I remember well those moments of little eyes trying to look under the door and little voices asking when I was coming out. It takes an effort and it will not happen by accident. But it

> is completely worth the effort to have the elements of the relationship with God that happen when you and He are having a moment.

We read in the New Testament book of James 4:8: *Come near to God and He will come near to you.* Begin to draw near to Him in your heart and in the quiet of your mind and He will miraculously meet you there to increase your faith with His love. This drawing near to God is a deliberate act of faith. It means that you believe that He will join you as He promised.

Spending time alone with God is also an act of obedience which is honored by discovering that there is so much to know about God. There is so much to know about His great love for you. This is, by necessity, a solitary journey. You and your family have a stronger and deeper harbor when you set out to lean into God when no one else can see or hear. Find a time and place of privacy and get closer to God.

The mysterious and almighty God wants to spend time with you just as you want to spend time with those that you love. This same God who sees all the secrets of your heart longs for you to know Him. There are many mysteries associated with God and many things about Him that we, as His children, cannot understand. But there is much about our heavenly Father that we can know and experience. He wants us to understand as much of Him as we possibly can. He delights in us. We are His children. God is love and love is God.

Think back again to the moment when you held your child for the very first time. If you were like me, you couldn't tear your eyes away from the sight of this tiny life in your arms. Whenever you held your child, you instinctively locked eyes and smiled. For just a moment, imagine that God is looking at you just like that. God is looking at you and smiling with an unspeakable joy because you are His precious treasure. If you think of God as a distant onlooker to the world or an impersonal Creator or a harsh taskmaster waiting to correct your mistakes, please know now that those perceptions have nothing to do with the One True God. He loves you. It is as simple as that.

Remember that even though the work of growing your faith is best done in private, faith must not be kept private. What good does a growing faith in a living God do if it is locked inside of you? The compassion and empathy that grows alongside faith helps humanity and secures your family only when you express it in words and deeds. This makes me think of photographs in the days before digital photography: faith is developed in private and then the evidence of it is shown in public. It is in this way that we serve our community, our family, and ourselves.

You are loved; your children are loved; your spouse and friends and siblings and coworkers and neighbors and the guy who runs the checkout counter at the grocery store are loved. All are loved beyond measure and reason by the God of the universe. God Almighty. El Shaddai. He loves you. This knowledge is the foundation of our faith.

Practical DIY Faith Tips

Faith in God has an incalculable value in a Harbor Home. On the next several pages we will examine some practical, concrete things that you can do to help develop the kind of faith that sustains your family. These are some actions taken by those who intentionally seek out a faith that creates the stability and security that we get from the deep water of the harbor. We will look at two areas of faith in any Harbor Home. Individual faith as it is developed inside you, and the faith of a family as they practice it together.

There are many ancient and time-honored disciplines that Christians have practiced that brought them to a deep and abiding faith in God. They will do the same for you. Some of the greatest of these teachers wrote down some practices that, when followed, can lead to a faith in God that will undergird your Harbor Home.

The following methods were prescribed by John Wesley (1703–1791). He was a great reformation minister in the Anglican Church (Church Of England) and the founder, along with his brother Charles, of the Methodist Movement. The largest modern denomination that emerged from that movement is the United Methodist Church.

- **Meditation:** Listening to and focusing on God. Many Christians believe that meditation differs from prayer in that it is an act of listening. Prayer can easily slip into a list of requests similar to a wish list to Santa Claus. Meditation is hearing what the Lord of Heaven and earth has to say to you. He wants to speak into your life and He wants you to take the time to listen. To grasp this, you must accept that God has a plan for you that is part of His overall plan for the universe. You must also accept that He will make His will known to you if you will take the time to meditate on Him. If you've never just been still and quiet while listening for God, try setting a timer on your watch or phone for five minutes. Sit in a quiet place alone and repeat softly a one-word prayer. Something like "peace" or "love" or, my favorite, *shalom.* If your thoughts drift to the laundry, meal planning, coworkers, gossip, or other distractions, set the timer again. Do this until you can meditate for five minutes. Then increase the time. Do not be fooled: the enemy will try to interrupt this process. Satan does not want you to draw near to God. He wants you to be tied in knots and feeling unsure of your value to God. Never forget God's love for you.

- **Prayer:** Pouring your heart out to God. God knows the secrets of our hearts. The Psalmist makes this very clear: *Would not God have discovered it, since he knows the secrets of the heart* (Psalm 44:21)? Since this is true, prayer should be an act of pure honesty with yourself and with God. Are you scared? Angry? Intimidated? Arrogant? Frustrated? Bitter? Discouraged? Elated? Hopeful? Confused? God knows all this. Go ahead and speak this to Him in prayer. There is no need for fancy religious words or over-the-top spiritual language. God speaks your language. He hears the heart, not the words. Pour your soul into your prayer and do not stop praying until you are satisfied that you have told it all and have held nothing back. Tell God your deepest fears, your greatest desire, your gravest disappointment. Ask Him to come and replace these overwrought emotions with His perfect peace. This is a peace that surpasses our understanding.
- ***Lectio Divina:*** This is a Latin phrase that translates to "divine reading." This is often defined as the practice

of reading the works of Christians who have a strong relationship with God and the gift of teaching His ways through writing. These books often take the form of someone telling about their faith's journey or a Bible study about certain aspects of God's divine nature. You don't have to read great scholarly works to be engaging in *lectio divina*. These deeper works can be really interesting and challenge your faith to move beyond a casual one, but the act of reading about God even in Christian fiction will help you keep your heart focused on Him. Words of faith give encouragement to your heart and mind and help you to see God in new ways. As time passes, you will be able to see how much your faith has grown through the act of *lectio divina*.

- **Reading Scripture:** The Holy Bible has no substitute, and there is no substitute for reading the words of God and planting them in your heart. The words of Scripture tell us about the God who is the same yesterday, today, and always and who is all love. God loves you. But how will you know this if you don't read and digest for yourself His own word? To paraphrase the great American author Mark Twain, If you do not read your Bible you are no better off than those who cannot read the Bible. There are literally hundreds of Bible reading plans available for free in print and on the internet. Choose one that seems to suit your habits and attention span. If you can listen or read for an hour or two a day then, by all means, jump into a one-year Bible reading plan. There were a few years when I was in my late twenties to early thirties when I devoted a lot of time to Scripture reading and read the Bible through in a year quite a few times. Now, I spend less time reading and more time meditating on what I read. Ask the Lord how He wants you to approach His word. He wants you to know Him, so He will show you how. Choose a reading plan that brings you joy and fulfillment. If you dread your Bible reading time and it feels like a chore, switch to something else but, whatever you do, continue to read the Bible.

- **Live Simply:** Gandhi famously said that we should all "live simply so that others may simply live". I've meditated on this seemingly straightforward quote many times and every time I think I've wrapped my heart and mind around it, the true depth of it slips away from me. Great faith leaders of the world's major religions (Gandhi was Hindu, The Dalai Lama is Buddhist, John Wesley a Christian) all encourage people to live a simple life: food, shelter, love of family and neighbor, using less while giving more. Living simply could mean arranging your life and expectations so that you have more time between scheduled obligations. Allow for margins in your home. Consider how many scheduled activities you and the others in your Harbor Home really need. Carefully choose a limited number of these to avoid the frantic pace of going from swim lessons to karate to music to scouts to book club to service club to church committees to cooking class and then home again to do the laundry, get showers and start it all again. Harbor Homes are meant to be joyful places free from constant chaos and frenetic pacing. Some seasonal chaos (read Christmas) is harder to avoid, but you are in charge of general scheduling.

> Be purposefully simple. Choose quality over quantity. Slow down and simplify a little. Own fewer clothes, wait longer between new cars, stay out of the glittery shopping emporiums that lure us into believing that we need more than we really do. Keep it simple.

There are a lot more items on John Wesley's list of personal practices for holiness including fasting, self-denial, and practicing silence regularly. This shorter list should get you started if you just need a nudge. Even if you are doing many of these things, a loving reminder of what we can do to draw closer to the God that loves us is never a bad idea. Consider taking on one or more of these practices for the benefit of your own faith and those around you.

Strengthening the Faith of Your Family

Faith in your own heart, helping your children develop their faith, practicing faith in a personal way—it all comes together to create a family faith that can be worked out together and will become a source of strength. Here are some examples of what your family can do to develop a strong faith together.

Worship

First of all, understand that the word "worship" is a verb. An action word. A word that implies doing. When you are truly going to worship, you are going to offer your love and devotion to God Almighty who created the heavens and the earth. There are many different thoughts, opinions, and styles of worship, and many personal expressions of faith. But honestly, God has a very short list of expectations concerning worship.

The Bible is quite clear: *God is spirit, and His worshipers must worship in spirit and in* truth (John 4:24). In other words, liturgical readings and formal practices that do not draw us into the spirit are not true worship. Neither is joyous hand clapping while jumping to the rhythm of a dynamic praise band unless you are worshiping in spirit and truth.

If you are not already doing so, worship with a congregation that is not just going through the motions of "traditional" or "contemporary" or "modern" worship. Worship regularly in a community that values worship and not just their rituals.

Even rituals that were instated very recently can be dead rituals. Don't assume that a great band, a dark worship space, and vivid videos mean that the Holy Spirit is present in the hearts of the worshipers. Equally, don't assume that stained glass, time-honored hymns, and scripted group prayer mean that the Holy Spirit is there. Worship in a carefully chosen community. Here are some thoughts about this.

Finding a Faith Community

As was mentioned earlier in this chapter, an individual can and should worship alone. But there is an important call to community worship that goes back thousands of years. The ancient Hebrews worshiped together, the earliest Christians did as well; they did this even when doing so jeopardized their lives. But consider it well. Your worship community is an important relationship, so be aware and make your selection with intention. There are a lot of factors to consider when you are looking for a group of believers.

Proximity: One of these factors is how close to your home it is. I know people who drive a long way to worship at the church they love, and if that works for you, that's great. But the hard truth is, if you have a long drive to get there you may not be as motivated to be active.

Meets Your Family Needs: If your parents or friends have a church that is important to them and they invite you, certainly go visit. But don't feel obligated to stay if it doesn't fit your family's needs. Instead, choose your community of worship by the way that community produces the fruit of the spirit and proclaims the true Gospel of Jesus Christ, His death on the cross, and His resurrection to atone for our sins.

By "the fruit of the spirit" I mean the list provided for us by Paul: *But the fruit of the Spirit is love, joy, peace, forbearance, kindness, goodness, faithfulness, gentleness, and self-control. Against such things there is no law* (Galatians 5:22–23). Look at that list closely:

- **Love:** Are the worshipers loving toward newcomers as well as each other? Do they love and respect their pastor? Are hurting people nurtured?
- **Joy:** Are smiles and laughter present in the halls and worship space?
- **Peace:** Are there constant conflicts about carpet color, lunch menus, or how to make pancakes?
- **Forbearance:** How much patience is displayed toward children, people struggling with addiction, church leadership?
- **Kindness:** This is self-explanatory and self-evident.
- **Goodness:** Bear in mind that "nice" is not the same as "good." People can appear to be nice, but being good goes

below the surface and is consistent with the gospel of Jesus Christ.

- **Faithfulness:** This is about remaining true to the Scriptures.
- **Gentleness:** This is easily recognized. People need to be treated with respect and consideration.
- **Self-Control:** This last one is the most challenging for us all, so be gracious in assessing this.

If you have a music preference, by all means, worship where you enjoy the music that is offered. But check out the other issues much more closely for they matter far more than the surface issue of which style of worship music we enjoy.

Make Regular Worship a Habit

By attending worship regularly I mean once a week, every week. I know that sounds unreasonable to many. I know several people who believe that five or six visits to their church per year, including Christmas Eve, constitutes regular attendance. But the Word of God asks us to remember to gather together. It is pretty straightforward *not giving up meeting together, as some are in the habit of doing, but encouraging one another* (Hebrews 10:25). Clearly, many of us have forgotten this teaching.

Many Americans say that they are "too busy" or even self-identify as "too lazy" to attend church on Sundays. The Pew Research Center is a great think tank that researches and analyses all things religion-related. There are a lot of interesting little tidbits that come to light about American worship practices. Particularly how seldom many Americans attend worship services even though they identify as Christians. ("Why Americans Go to Religious and Church Services," 2020)

I understand that on Sunday mornings getting out of the house seems inconvenient. When you work full time, even if weekend hours are not included, Sunday seems like a day to relax or do other things. To resolve this very real issue, two of our children take their children to a five o'clock pm worship service on Sundays.

They spend the entire day together relaxing and playing as a family, then wind down the day by worshiping. They attend a large urban church where there is no particular or unspoken dress code, the children's education program is run by child-friendly people who know the Bible and passionately pass on the faith. The worship experience beckons in the Holy Spirit.

The evening ends for their families with a treat such as a drive-through fast-food meal. This sort of arrangement can work for you too. Be creative. Research the options in your area. Even if you don't live in a major metropolitan area, you should be able to locate a worship schedule that allows your family to participate. This allows worship to be a regular part of each week, and your Harbor Homes will be blessed.

Summary of Chapter Two

The culture outside of our homes is similar in many ways to the Graveyard of the Atlantic. Opposing currents batter and compete with one another for control. Our world now, as it always has been, is full of turmoil and confusion. Like the waters of this coast, the world is unreliable and requires much from us when we set out upon it.

It is very helpful to have the tools we need to navigate the rough water as well as a safe harbor to which we can return. A deep faith upholding you and your family is like a deep water harbor beneath a large ocean-going vessel. It will hold you safely and keep you from running aground. Invest in this. It will take time and attention, but you will never regret it

Consistently doing what the faithful have done throughout the centuries to build your faith will create for you and your family the deep water in which you can thrive and be at peace. Encouraging your children to develop faith that is their own and grows as they grow is a great work of love for you.

Questions for Further Discussion or Deeper Thinking

1. When did you first realize that you wanted to have a relationship with God? Try to remember as much detail as you can. What did you say to yourself? What did you hear God say to you? What was your response to God?
2. What are the most important elements of your faith now and why?
3. What one thing do you want to add to your faith practices but haven't done so yet? How will you work it into your life?
4. How do you think your children view your family's faith? Would they say that faith is very important to your family or not terribly important?
5. Describe your prayer time as it concerns your family. What and when do you pray?

Chapter Three

THE INLET: WHO IS COMING INTO YOUR HARBOR?

The righteous choose their friends carefully, for the way of the wicked leads them astray.

Proverbs 12:26

The Inlet at Ocracoke is a relatively calm, safe opening to the ocean. That makes it pretty special because the inlets at other villages along the Outer Banks are turbulent, unpredictable, and, at times, dangerous. Ocracoke's safe inlet has influenced the village tremendously by allowing free entry from the shipping and travel lanes of the ocean to the safe harbor of Silver Lake at Ocracoke Island.

Owing to the safe inlet and deep water harbor, Ocracoke and the nearby island village of Portsmouth, now abandoned, were once two of the biggest ports in North Carolina. Goods and people flowed in and out constantly. Fishermen and sailors, ship captains and crew, carpenters, all manner of ocean-going tradesmen and . . . pirates.

Many people know about Blackbeard, the notorious pirate whose given name was Edward Teach. He was eventually caught and killed in the waters just off Ocracoke by a British naval officer named Maynard. Blackbeard is a well-known character in Ocracoke lore and is given a good bit of attention by local businesses. On Ocracoke, you will find a Blackbeard museum and a small inlet into the harbor called Teach's Hole. A local craft brewery named their business in honor of the infamous pirate and a couple of the inns have names that give a nod to this notorious local legend.

Blackbeard was not, by any means, the only pirate who sought out the protection offered by Ocracoke's natural shelter. Calico Jack, another pirate famous of the era, enjoyed the safety of this harbor. So did the two most famous female pirates Anne Bonney and Mary Reed. There were others whose names have been lost to history.

It is hard for most of us to imagine the evil that pirates of the late seventeenth century and well into the eighteenth century brought to coastal towns as well as ships at sea. These days we have romanticized pirates calling them "swashbucklers," "buccaneers," and such. We imagine them wearing Hollywood-type costumes while getting the better of foolish, arrogant merchants and inept sea captains in well-scripted battles. We have made them into admired folk heroes. We think of them as handsome and bold, brave and clever.

The truth is quite different. Pirates were dangerous armed criminals. They were vicious and violent people who lived on stolen wealth and were proud of it. They were wicked and felt entitled to take anything they saw. Then, after stealing what they wanted, without any regret, they cruelly killed, tortured, or imprisoned the rightful owners of the property. Think about the drug lords running the cartels of our day and the number of people who have been killed and viciously attacked by them. Think about the leaders of violent street gangs who openly encourage killing people and destroying property as a means of gaining acceptance into the gang. This is who pirates really were. There is no glory in this. They were criminals without conscience embracing the lowest instincts of humanity.

In your Harbor Home, strive to allow entry only to individuals and groups who carry with them a positive influence. A safe inlet is going to be attractive to everyone including those who do not have good motives for being there. If you have created a home in which people feel welcome, you will have the most popular home in town. Everyone wants to feel welcome. However, it is important to remember that there are those who will want to come into your home and are able to cause discord and chaos very quickly. Once negativity has begun, if it is not stopped quickly, it will bring much unhappiness to your home. Choose all friends and companions very carefully.

As a young mother, I would remind my children that I would know them by their friends. I emphasized the importance of having companions that obeyed their own parents and spoke politely to others; friends who were kind and generous and knew how to play without doing irresponsible things that could get someone hurt. The ability to choose companions well is a good skill to have.

When you choose companions, you are really choosing who will influence you. The people you spend time with are going to direct the course of your days far more than you realize. Let me give an example: When I was in my forties I met a new friend who, when feeling surprised, would say, "good googly moogly!" Up until she and I became friends, I would, in similar circumstances, say, "good grief!" or "good heavens!" But guess what I say now? I now use the expression my friend taught me. She impacted my speech patterns just because we spent time together. We are all affected in many ways by those who are around us the most.

In all the young lives I have been privileged to touch, I could clearly see how friends and companions shaped one another. Fashion, speech, hobbies, habits, attitudes, opinions, and more. Many parents panic when they begin to see that their teens and tweens are using slang words and choosing clothing that is influenced by the peer group and not by the parents.

Take notice: God created us to live in community. He wants us to be in each other's lives and to strengthen one another. He sent Jesus so that we could be impacted by His influence and His life. Our Lord longs for us to impact our community with the love of Jesus and to affect those who surround us.

It is not necessarily a bad thing for your children or you to be influenced by others. A friend who is a very good cook can inspire you to improve your own kitchen skills. A friend with a positive outlook can help you to look on the sunny side. A friend who goes to church every week without fail can encourage you to attend worship more regularly. A friend who speaks patiently to her children can help you to become more patient as a mother.

I have known several women in my life that when I look at them I say to myself, "when I grow up I want to be just like her." They offer a new way of looking at an issue or give me the courage to try something I have never done before. Many wonderful women of God have helped me overcome fears that held me in their grip all of my life simply because I was watching how they overcame their own fears.

These are the sort of people you want to have in your harbor. Let the brave, the cheerful, the inspiring, the hopeful come through the inlet. Seek out people that you admire and let them influence you. I used to hear a teacher tell her students, "Show me your friends and I will show you your future." This is not just a saying for young people. Use this advice to shape your own future.

You may have heard it said that you are the average of the five people you are around the most. This quote is typically attributed to motivational speaker Jim Rohn. But there are some human behaviorists who say that his statement does not go far enough. There are now some who believe that we are not only the average of those five people but also of the five people that those people are with most often even if we do not know those others. The point is we are a wide community in which each life touches and leaves an imprint. Our joyful friend makes us more joyful and so we then pass on the joy to someone that our joyful friend doesn't even know! Influence travels far and wide.

There are several elements that you can learn to be aware of as you choose those that you will allow to influence your home. It is helpful to be able to state clearly to yourself reasons why a person will or will not be a positive influence. In this way, you are not relying only on your intuition or emotions but on criteria that you have thought through in advance. Here are some suggestions for how you can decide about positive companions. Perhaps you have others.

How To Recognize Positive Companions

The Words Chosen

One key component to choosing friends is to listen to the words they use to communicate. Luke 6:45 says, *The mouth speaks what the heart is full of,* meaning that you really can know what is going on in someone's heart by listening to how they speak. Sometimes when someone is in real distress they may use language they are later embarrassed by or they may occasionally speak with more anger or passion than they typically do, but listen to how people express themselves most of the time.

I took an Old Testament course many years ago and the wise professor explained that when God spoke the universe into existence He was sending His spirit out to create the earth in the form of His breath with sound. This is what words are: breath with sound. He went on to say that since we are created in the image of God our words are also how our spirit goes out to the world. It is our words that indicate more than anything else what our spirits, hearts, and minds contain. When we speak, we are sharing our spirit.

Without getting too graphic, let me recount the story of my son coming home from kindergarten with a deeply troubling question. "Mama, what is a ***** *****?" I could feel the blood draining out of my head. I had not heard that phrase until I was in my mid-teens, and I absolutely have never ever said it. Here stood my adorable little blond-haired, blue-eyed boy who knew it was a terrible phrase, but he had heard it at school and he had no clue what it meant. So he asked me. Thank God.

I prayed for composure and responded with as much neutrality in my face as possible. "There are some words," I began, "that are so bad and so ugly that they have no meaning at all. They are just bad and ugly. This is one of those."

"That's what I thought," he said. He went on to tell me the whole scenario, and I was really sad that there were children in his class who lived with such language in their homes.

"You know," I pointed out when he finished, "every family has different rules that they live by. In our family, one of our rules is that we choose our words with care and make sure that they are kind and make other people feel good inside. You know that I don't use ugly words, neither do your grandparents or anyone in our family. It is how we do things. Some families think that using those words is fine, but in our family, we use only words that God thinks are nice. So you don't have to worry about those words. Just remind yourself that in our family we don't use them. How does that sound to you?"

The relief was evident on his face. That simple assurance that in our family we have a plan in place to avoid hurtful speech was all that he really required that day. He just needed a reminder that our home is a harbor and those kinds of words are not permitted. People who habitually use repulsive language are simply not allowed through the inlet. They exist out in the rough waters of kindergarten but not in our harbor.

Words are how our spirits reach out; words show the world what is in our hearts and souls; words matter. I consider a person's way of expressing themselves in words a very important clue to how good a friend they would be and how willing I am to allow them to enter the harbor of our home. Certainly, there are other criteria, but people demonstrate their character pretty quickly with their words.

When my children were small I taught them a modified version of an old saying. It went like this: *Sticks and stones may break my bones but words will break my heart.* I used this as a way to help them learn not only to use words carefully but also to be careful about how much power you give the words of other people.

Words go into your heart and mind as well as out of your heart and mind. Be very careful of the words you allow to flow in either direction. There is a real risk of having your heart broken if you give too much weight to the words that others speak to you. There are times to listen carefully to others and times to set those words to one side without giving them any room to influence what you know to be true.

Words matter. Use them and choose them wisely. Listen to the words that others use and decide whether or not you want to allow them to come into your harbor. You do not have to take in every word spoken to you. Compare the words that others speak to you to the words that the Lord speaks to you. If those words are not the same, choose the Lord over the people around you.

Respect for Faith and Values

During my years as a minister to young people, I taught an in-depth lesson each year about the importance of choosing friends well. Using Daniel and his friends as a springboard we would discuss how the friendship between Daniel, Hananiah, Mishael, and Azariah (known also by their Babylonian names Shadrach,

Meshach, and Abednego) strengthened each of their lives. This bond of friendship built each one up; they encouraged one another to remain faithful to the teachings of their childhood.

I have often wondered how much more difficult it would have been for any one of them alone. Would they have had the strength to stand up to the king's men and insist that their food be different? They had customs and habits that differed from the Babylonian boys in the king's training school. Would they have been able to withstand the pressure to stop praying to their God when ordered to do so had they not had the support of their shared faith? These were remarkable young men who shaped and sharpened and upheld each other for decades. This is friendship at its best.

Their earliest teachings helped those young men to achieve great things in the name of God. They became trusted advisors not only to their own exiled people but to the king who had taken them into captivity. Daniel's friends were very important to him. The friendships that are part of your harbor home are just as important. Your friends and those of your children are influential to the overall quality of your life. Choose friends like Daniel. Be a friend like Daniel.

How do you feel after you have been with your friend?

Some people have a remarkable ability to see the best in us and then point it out so that we can see it too. They naturally lift us up with encouragement, positive comments, jokes, and pleasant conversation. The affirming influence that this friend has on your outlook and your mood last far beyond the time that you spend together. When you leave, you feel at least as good as you did when you arrived. You are, in fact, a better person each time you are with this friend. Not everyone leaves you feeling this way.

Be thoughtful about how you feel after you've spent some time with a friend. Are you agitated, angry or frustrated? Are you drained, tired, grumpy? Or are you happy and optimistic? Do you feel better about yourself? Did your conversation make you feel respected? Did you leave with a vaguely off-balance kind of feeling or do you leave feeling lighthearted? Do you think later of things you wish you had said or left unsaid? Just take note of how you feel. If your time with your friend is consistently not good, consider that they don't really need to be a part of your harbor home.

Be especially aware of this with your younger children. They may not know how to tell you if their friend is being critical or hurtful. Observe their demeanor after they have been with a friend. Are they happy or not? Notice how they value themselves in the hours and days after a visit.

Children can be cruel, bossy, and opinionated. If your child's friend is often critical of your child's clothing, body shape, skill at games or sports, or anything else and your child's sense of self is declining, find a way to limit contact or eliminate it altogether. But remember to be gentle about their friend, because the tendency will be for your child to get defensive about their friend. Talk openly with your child about how they feel while they are with this friend without being negative. If you must eliminate contact, do so quietly and calmly without making a scene or calling much attention to the decision.

If you are concerned about a friend your child or teen wants to spend time with, invite them to be at your house with your supervision until you feel confident about the relationship. Rejecting a companion without spending some time with them is unfair and could put a rift between you and your child. As the parent, you can just stay nearby. Be a friendly host offering snacks or activities. Be kind even if you have your doubts about the friendship. Maybe you can be the adult that shapes a young life.

What kind of activities do you and your friend engage in?

I have had some wonderful friends in my life and together we have done a lot of fun things. Sometimes we do things that we all really love and sometimes we all go along with what one enjoys. I have friends that love hiking as much as I do, and we go out and explore the trails in our area. These same friends often enjoy kayaking and other outdoorsy things. We will throw our kayaks in the water and paddle until we feel like turning around.

I also have friends who love to shop for clothes. This is something I choose to do only when I absolutely have to and, even then, I don't really enjoy it very much. But I have learned from my shopper friends a lot about choosing attractive clothing, finding bargains, and completing an outfit. So now, I am usually appropriately dressed and accessorized whatever the occasion. Even though I'm engaged in an activity that is less than thrilling to me, I'm always grateful when I get an invitation to go shopping with my stylish friends. We have good conversations and, in addition, I am actually getting better at doing something that I really do need to do with the help of friends gifted in that area. They make me look and feel better every time.

I have friends who like to do things that I am afraid to do. Like ride horses, go rock climbing, or ride roller coasters. But I am afraid of horses and heights. Actually, I am pretty much terrified of them. Even so, I have done each of these things with friends. I would not go out of my way to do any of this on my own, but through trusting my friends I have had new experiences that enriched my life.

Trying out new and scary activities keeps our minds sharp and adds a bit of adventure to our lives. Try out new things with a friend. You might find that you really enjoy it, or, if not, you might have a good story to tell. When you have done something scary and lived to tell the tale, you may find that you gain confidence and strength.

I know people who enjoy going places and doing things that make me so uncomfortable and ill at ease that I simply don't participate. These people are still in my circle of acquaintances and certainly, I am polite and I enjoy superficial conversation with them whenever we meet or are at an event together but, strictly speaking, they are not really part of my harbor. I will not be lured or coerced into joining an activity that feels wrong or unsafe or sketchy in any way.

For example, I do not like a bar atmosphere at all and I never have. I don't mind the kind of bar in a restaurant or hotel, but the stand-alone kind of bar is not my cup of tea. So when I am invited to go to this sort of bar, I smile politely and decline the invitation. I feel no need to give a lecture about why. I just do not go. There are other invitations that I decline in the same way. You can do this too. Politely decline an invitation that would put you in a situation that makes you uncomfortable for whatever reason. You do not have to explain, just politely say no.

Be aware of what activities you are comfortable doing and don't join in if you are not comfortable. Even if you feel pressured to do so. If necessary, practice saying no to an invitation. It is okay for you to refuse to do something or go somewhere when you are uncomfortable. Being a good friend together in a harbor means that everyone makes their own decisions. If you have people in your harbor who won't take no for an answer when they invite you to do something that you don't want to do, then they don't need to stay in your harbor. Remember: your harbor belongs to you.

Looking at this from the opposite angle, if your friend does not want to go somewhere or participate in an activity and you really want them to, accept their answer graciously. You may not understand why they don't want to join in, but it is okay. They have a reason that makes sense to them, and you can let them do what they wish without putting pressure on them or placing them in the awkward position of arguing their point. If your friend says no, just let it go.

Your teens can be taught this concept. Here is how I know: my wonderful husband was a teenager in the late 1960s when it was becoming fashionable to smoke marijuana. He knew that many of his classmates and friends were doing this, and he knew that it was illegal and not safe. He wanted nothing to do with drugs of any kind. So he made up his mind long before he was offered his first experience with marijuana that he would refuse it. He wasn't sure what he would say or what he would do, but he knew that he would decline any offer of this.

It wasn't long before his resolve was tested. One night, in a movie theater with friends, my husband was offered a joint. He says now that he was glad that he had decided ahead of time to refuse because he didn't have to make a decision under pressure.

He passed the joint along without a word. He didn't even pretend to smoke it.

He realized then that he needed to make an additional decision. And this time it was a bit more challenging. He knew that if his friends were making decisions to do things like smoke marijuana they were probably going to do other things that would be just as dangerous. He knew he needed to find a new group of friends. And he did.

How do you behave?

I used to know two boys who were delightful and funny and smart and altogether wonderful. Until they were together. When they were together they were almost certainly headed for trouble. They were young enough that the kind of trouble they headed for was not life-altering, but they did things together that they would never have done alone and had no business doing at all. I never figured out why but it was nearly guaranteed that if those two were together something bad was going to happen.

If you find that you do or say things in the presence of one friend or set of friends that you would not do or say in the presence of other friends, consider why. Especially if you are sorry or embarrassed later on. Think about how much you complain when you are with one friend over another. Consider how much gossip you share about mutual friends or acquaintances. If you have a tendency to use profane language with one friend but not with another friend, think about which group makes you feel more proud to be with. Which group would you rather be part of? Which group would you rather be identified with? Which group has life goals that are similar to yours?

You may notice that you feel as though you are a better person when you are with one friend than you are with another. This matters. How you speak and behave when you are with someone reflects how you are influencing each other. Decide on the kind of person that you want to be and choose companions that support that. And be the companion that supports your friend in being the person they want to be.

Invisible Invaders

The Media in Your Harbor

Everywhere we turn we are bombarded with messages from some form of media. Videos, music, photographs, social pages, websites, clickbait, twenty-four-seven news cycles. It seems that there is no way to get even a moment of respite from all the external noise. These messages are at least as influential on you and your family as the companions you allow in. In our culture, we are, literally, never free from the constant barrage of influencers asking for our and our children's attention, support, help, and, ultimately, money.

Most of us have become so accustomed to all the media noise that we don't really notice it. The racket goes in one ear and out the other without slowing down in our brains long enough to make an impact. Or so we think. In fact, the onslaught of information has an enormous influence on how we behave, live, and think. These messages that come at us from our computer screens, tablets, phones, and televisions are now the basis of how most people perceive the world; how they perceive family; how they perceive God and how they perceive Christ. Be very mindful about what media comes into your home.

One of the greatest concerns that I have in this ongoing media blitz is the fact that we do not know the origin of the messages we are receiving. Who is speaking to us and sending all the information that we are taking in? Where does the information come from? Who has created the messages we are hearing day in and day out? We very often don't know and, it seems, we don't care. But we should care. The source matters.

Communication and body language experts have known for decades that 90 percent of all communication is non-verbal. In other words, we give and receive a great deal of information by the way we gesture with our hands or our tone of voice or our facial expressions, or from our relationship with whoever we are speaking with.

Suppose someone shares with you a piece of outrageous gossip about someone you both know. What happens when you believe the outrageous story, pass it along and then you find out that it never really happened? It is too late by then. You have harmed someone's reputation. You have harmed your relationship. This happened because you listened to an unreliable source. The source of the story is important.

If you are speaking with a seven-year-old who is telling you about a tree that fell down in your neighborhood you understand immediately what perspective the story is coming from. You know that a seven-year-old can certainly know if a tree fell down, but the other details are coming from a child's point of view which is different from an adult's.

Consider now that you are hearing the same event recalled by a neighbor on the far end of the neighborhood. From them, you get yet another perception. They know the tree fell but only because they heard it. When you hear the story from the neighbor who lives in the house next to the fallen tree you are hearing yet another experience. They saw it, heard it, and felt the ground shake because of the impact. Each of these versions comes with an emphasis on different details and a slightly different way of looking at the event. But one of the versions is the most reliable.

When you know who is telling the story as well as why they are telling the story then you have a context that helps with your understanding. When we hear news and other current event stories from the big media corporations and social media community we are almost never certain of the source of our information. And, as I have said, the source matters.

All these things matter because what you listen to is influencing your thinking, your responses, your opinions, and your understanding of your community. It is possible to be an informed citizen while remaining true to our faith and maintaining common sense. Spend more time moving in and around your community and your neighbors than you do watching and listening to media that is telling you about your community and your neighbors.

Other media influences in your home are images in the form of magazines or websites. Many of these are permeated with sexuality that is designed to destroy a healthy concept of sex and replace it with a viewpoint that is harmful to marriages and the innocence of young minds. It is your responsibility to maintain purity in your home.

It is nearly impossible to keep these images from influencing you and your family when you are away from home, but you can refuse them entry into your own harbor. Keep even so-called "soft" pornography away from the sensitive minds of young children and the hormonally charged minds of older children.

The best way to do this is to maintain an organic and ongoing conversation about the realities of intimate human interaction. Your children want to learn about these personal things from you. Make sure they know that the images they see in advertisements are airbrushed and edited so that there is no reality left in them. Make it clear that you are available to talk about anything that they are curious about.

Children know what is acceptable and what is not by what you allow in your home. If you calmly and systematically reject oversexualized images, they will know that there is another, more healthy way to show what humans are like. Protect their hearts and minds as long as you can so that when they encounter inappropriate circumstances they have a clear knowledge of a more sound and healthy way to view humanity.

Anytime you can see the world and your community through the eyes of Christ instead of through the eyes of mass media you and your children are better off emotionally and mentally. You are more likely to be able to truly love your neighbor if you see them face to face instead of listening to the television news tell you about your neighbor. Assume good things until you have seen otherwise with your own eyes.

Reporters can only report accurately what they have seen and heard. Everything else is speculation and opinion. Be careful about how much time you spend listening to our highly biased news reporters. Stop watching or listening if you begin to feel tense or angry or frightened or hopeless. God is still on the throne and Jesus is still on His right hand. Be prepared, be aware, be balanced and well.

So here is the bottom line concerning all media in your Harbor Home: limit, limit, limit. Pay enough attention to know what the current events are, but be cautious about listening to how the big news outlets interpret these events. They are not fortune-tellers with crystal balls that predict the future, nor can they read the motives of every public figure that has a sound bite in that day's news cycle.

Your Influence in the Harbor

Know Your Power

So far in this chapter, we have been addressing ways to manage the atmosphere of your personal space. It is important to notice that we are often in someone else's space. How we behave and speak when we are guests in another harbor influences our community as a whole. Our behavior also, of course, determines our reputation in the community. Knowing how to present the best version of ourselves is important because we are representing so much more than just ourselves.

Our words and actions can either cause harm or create joy. We have the power to build or destroy whole organizations as well as individuals with just our words. The impact of what we choose to say and how we choose to say it cannot be overstated. The level to which we encourage others will determine how welcome we are in a workplace or social setting.

We each have our own personality that is formed through cultural influences, upbringing, experiences, education, and certain mysterious genetic quirks that are way beyond my scope of understanding. Our personalities can be used to be a positive influence on those around us if we look beyond ourselves and our own desires. By setting aside our natural selfish nature and embracing generosity we become better versions of ourselves and our personalities grow around this nature.

There is a marvelous legend about William Booth, the founder of The Salvation Army. The exact details seem to have been lost to history, but my favorite version of this story has this event occurring on Christmas of 1910. In those days, the quickest way to communicate was by telegram, and the cost of telegrams was based on the number of words in the message. The Salvation Army has always emphasized frugality and loving people in all walks of life. This story, paraphrased by me, highlights both of these:

It seems that William Booth wanted to send a telegram to each of his officers around the world to remind them of their mission. To do this in a cost-effective way he sent a telegram consisting of one word. Only one word. The word he chose was *others*. The mission of this Christ-centered organization can be summed up in the word "others." What a beautiful way to live in our community.

Summary of Chapter Three

Our Harbors have inlets. The inlets allow others to come in and us to go out. The extent to which we choose to live with our hearts and minds focused on others and on the love of Jesus Christ will be the greatest determining factor of love, joy, and unity as we work through the ongoing process of creating our Harbor Homes.

Be mindful of who comes in through the inlet. Pirates who want to rob you of your peace and joy will try to sneak into your welcoming harbor so keep watch. You have the power to move uninvited drama away from the shelter of your cove. You also have the power to keep yourself from being the source of drama. Hold a steady course as you choose friends and as you become a friend. Maintain a close eye on who is allowed to influence your minds with their words. Maintain a close watch on your own words. Dedicate your harbor to the needs of others. Keep the channel clear.

Questions for Discussion or Deeper Thinking

1. Think about the three friends that you spend the most time with. How did you become friends and why do you remain friends?
2. How have your friends influenced you?
3. What would your friends say is the best part of being your friend?
4. What are some ways that you can live out the concept of "others" in your immediate family that would require a sacrifice on your part?
5. What habits can you develop that would help you to be a positive influence in your community, school, or workplace?
6. What one word can sum up your life mission?

Chapter Four

LIGHT STATIONS AND HARBOR LIGHTS GUARDIANS AND GUIDES

When Jesus spoke again to the people, He said, "I am the light of the world. Whoever follows me will never walk in darkness, but will have the light of life."

John 8:12

Lighthouses are fascinating to most people. There is something dependable and trustworthy about them. We think of lighthouses in remote seaside locations holding strong against fierce seas and ferocious winds. We admire their ability to remain standing, some for centuries, through all types of weather. Lighthouses seem romantic and mysterious and, somehow, wise. The large, round towers or the great, square houses that stand on tall stilts above the water impress us. They rise over the land and shine out to the sea telling everyone, "Come this way! It's safer over here!"

Some of my favorite stories from childhood have a lighthouse as the central element. One of my earliest memories was someone reading to me *The Little Red Lighthouse and the Great Gray Bridge* by Hildegard H. Swift, illustrated by Lynd Ward, published in 1942. If you have not read this book, get it immediately and snuggle up with your favorite young person and read it aloud.

This book was especially fascinating to me because when I was a child we lived in the suburbs of New York City. We often went over the George Washington Bridge (the great gray bridge of the story's title) and Mother would encourage us to look for the little red lighthouse. It is still there today on Riverside Drive in the Upper West Side of Manhattan. I was always so certain that I saw it, and I would spend the rest of the car ride wondering what living in a lighthouse would be like. I still wonder.

Even now, I am immediately drawn to historical mysteries which occurred at lighthouses, or novels set at lighthouses. Even the lighthouse scene in *Harry Potter And The Philosopher's Stone* by J.K. Rowling lights up my imagination more than the great castle of Hogwarts. I just love lighthouses. Maybe you do too.

Thinking about lighthouses always makes me think about the keepers of the lighthouses. The men and women and their families who lived in typically isolated areas and who faithfully, constantly, carefully tended to the light day after lonely day. They remained true in freezing cold sleet, blazing hot humidity, hurricane-force winds and rain, and all other forces of the weather.

I imagine myself bravely climbing a black wrought iron spiral staircase, toolkit in my hand. Up I go to trim the big braided rope wick and polish the lenses so that the light could shine to all those mariners that I would never meet. At the top of my tower, I imagine breathing in the fresh salt air and gazing out at the vast ocean and wondering what was beyond the horizon.

Isn't it romantic? Ah well, it was not to be. Since a lighthouse stays still I would probably be fine, but my experience with life on the ocean is limited to offshore fishing with my husband while being seasick the entire time. Seriously. The entire time. Boating on the lake is better for me. Kayaking on the lake is better still. But a lighthouse . . . ahhh.

I have to confess to being a bit disappointed, but not really surprised, to learn that of the approximately seven hundred lighthouses in the United States only one has an actual keeper who turns the light on at dusk and off again at dawn. That one lighthouse is The Boston Lighthouse. Due to its significance as the oldest lighthouse in America, The United States Congress decreed that it should always be manned by a dedicated keeper. All the others, every single one, are automated.

At the Outer Banks of North Carolina, the only lighthouse keepers are volunteers who love the lighthouses or National Park Service Rangers who share the history of these very special places with the tourists who, like me, can't get enough. They don't get to work the light, but they appreciate the importance and the courage of those who did it for centuries. The lives of those keepers are honored every day.

Automated or not, lighthouses and light stations remain an integral part of a complex system of navigational aids. Each lighthouse has, within its region, a different nighttime flash and rotate pattern. Mariners at night know each lighthouse by how quickly the bright beacon flashes then turns. This gives them a visual reference for their global navigation.

Lighthouses also have a distinctive paint scheme or structural element in order to be recognizable by day. These imposing towers in clear weather can be seen fourteen miles offshore and they have kept an unknowable number of ships safe and on course as they travel. Commercial interests, private vessels, and passenger ships depend on them now as ever.

Along that section of the North Carolina coast known as The Outer Banks, there are five working lighthouses that are the objects of much admiration. One of these is the famed Hatteras Lighthouse, which is the tallest lighthouse in North America. It has the signature black and white candy-striped paint pattern that many around the world recognize.

The youngest of the five lighthouses, first lit on December 1, 1875, is the Currituck Beach Light. It is also the northernmost of the Outer Banks light stations. It is a red brick tower that is similar in size and dimension to the next light station south as you travel along the North Carolina coast.

That light is the Bodie Island Lighthouse (pronounced like *body*) and it has black and white alternating horizontal stripes to identify it by day. It was completed in 1872 and protects the area surrounding Oregon Inlet. It was the last of the five Outer Banks lighthouses to be renovated and opened to tourists. As you make your way south on NC Highway 12 heading along the Cape Hatteras National Seashore, you can stop and visit this lighthouse and the historic artifacts in the small museum on site.

The smallest of these light towers, by far, is the Ocracoke Lighthouse, which proudly and diligently works as the second oldest operating lighthouse in the United States. Its light is set slightly off-center on the top of a seventy-five-foot tower. Since 1823, this light has not ever failed in its mission to guide ships through the Ocracoke Inlet into the Pamlico Sound and then to the Ocracoke Harbor. It is painted a gleaming white and sits in the village of Ocracoke with a wooden walkway beside it inviting visitors to approach and look.

At Ocracoke Island, NC the light of the lighthouse is special. It is different from the others in more than just its size and paint scheme. It is a harbor light. This light that denotes the harbor does not flash or rotate. It shines a steady, unblinking light into the darkness. So while the other lights are flashing and rotating, the Ocracoke light simply lights the way home to the harbor. It welcomes all who will come to be safe and at peace.

A Lighthouse For You

In your Harbor Home, a lighthouse is a guide or guardian that offers support and wise counsel when you need it. They give you encouragement, advice, instructions, tips, and lifehacks. And recipes if you are really blessed. A lighthouse in your life is a benefit to you and to your family. With a lighthouse nearby there is no need to muddle through as you work to figure out the difficult paths of the narrow channel. There is help and guidance for navigating the journey.

In our Harbor Home, we have always wholeheartedly embraced the idea of having lighthouses. My husband and I have also been privileged to serve as lighthouses, but that does not mean that we no longer need them ourselves. We are deeply grateful to the people who do life with us and are lighthouses that shine light for us. None of us outgrow the need for mature friends who are trustworthy and wise.

Those who serve us in this way are usually people we know well. But not always. Sometimes they are people we meet who have special expertise that we need at the moment. They tend to be older or wiser; usually both. They are willing to be the ones we turn to when we need them. We may need them for perspective on a problem, advice in a predicament, a sounding board as we work through a decision, correction when we make mistakes, comfort when we mourn, cheering while we strive, or another manner of support. But when we need counsel, we turn to those who can give it.

I can say right now with great confidence that you need a lighthouse in your life. Everyone does. The most independent and self-assured person needs a lighthouse. Those who are accomplished, successful, intelligent, energetic, and brave all need at least one lighthouse. Those who are struggling and lonely, frustrated and frightened really need a lighthouse. You and I each need a lighthouse. Why then, do we seem to resist the idea of having one?

Why You Need a Lighthouse

Perhaps we push back against having a lighthouse because we believe that if we need one we are admitting to ourselves and to others that we don't know everything that we need to know to run our lives. Nobody likes to seem as though they are incapable of taking care of their own business. We want our family, friends, and neighbors to think that we can manage our money, our children, our housework, our careers, and our relationships perfectly well.

We can do it with ease and grace day in and day out. And, usually, we can.

It is true that very often the running of our lives is pretty straightforward and we can manage things well. Until we can't. And that is when we need to turn to a lighthouse that we trust. But we want everyone to think that we are fine. We're fine, thanks. We are embarrassed to be anything else.

We are fine and can manage well until we make one or more very large and unwise purchases such as a new car or a house that we know we can't afford. When we are staring bankruptcy in the face we need a lighthouse to show us how to get back on a strong financial track. Debt that you can get into in thirty minutes can take thirty years to get out of. Literally. The right lighthouse will be able to help you make good financial decisions that protect you and your family. They can encourage you to live within your means.

We are fine and we can manage our homes pretty well until the new baby we expected is twins and getting organized is beyond us. We are exhausted and frustrated in addition to being excited. We need a lighthouse to help us negotiate the changes, give us sound management advice and help us until we get there. A good lighthouse will help you learn new ways to order your day, organize your closets, stock your pantry, and may even come to take care of the babies while you get some sleep.

We are fine and our marriages are fine until the largest wage earner in the family loses the job that provided that paycheck. We are terrified. We may be angry. A lighthouse can help us continue to love each other until our marriage is off the rocks. This is one of the greatest stressors a marriage can have, and a trusted guide is worth their weight in gold at such a time. They can help you steady the ship, mitigate your fear and suggest ways to retool your resume and get back to business.

In general, a lighthouse in your life can help you navigate the sandbars that are going to appear. No one is immune to complications that can run your family aground onto a rock-strewn coast. Everyone needs a lighthouse that can help avoid the sandbars whenever possible and show a way to get off the sandbar once you've hit one. You need a lighthouse. Even if you don't want one, you need one.

We don't want advice. We don't want to need advice. We especially don't want to need advice when we really need advice. We even more especially don't want to need advice when we are beginning to crash on the rocks and it is our own fault.

It is a cruel irony of the human spirit that we feel compelled to turn away from advice when we need it the most. But this is not the way of Christ. It is not the way of community. It is not how we do life in the harbor. In the harbor, we look for the lighthouse when we are lost.

At the risk of repeating myself, I'm going to repeat myself. Learning to accept wise counsel is a life skill and an art that does not come naturally to most of us. As a rule, we like to think that we know everything we need to know, thank you very much, and we don't want advice. This attitude is not scriptural nor does it help you through life.

Thinking about all this reminds me of a story I heard a long time ago. If you haven't heard it, it's sort of funny and I've paraphrased it here. This story is told as though it is true although I seriously doubt it. In fact, let's assume it is not.

On a dark and stormy night, a US aircraft carrier was cruising in Canadian waters when it spotted a vessel directly in front of them. They were certainly going to collide unless one of the two adjusted their course. The US Naval Captain got on his radio and ordered the oncoming vessel to change course 15 degrees north in order to avoid a collision. Astonishingly, the other vessel refused and told the captain that he should change his course fifteen degrees south to avoid a collision. The irate captain shouted back that he was a captain in the United States Navy and demanded that the vessel divert immediately. The Canadian responded that he was a Petty Officer 2nd Class in the Canadian Navy, and he suggested that the aircraft carrier divert. Totally livid, the US captain hollered "This is an aircraft carrier! Change course immediately!" The Canadian responded, "This is a lighthouse. Your call."

I want to reiterate that I did not create this story, and I don't believe that it is true but rather it is a joke or an urban legend. I know a few naval officers and more than a few competent off-shore mariners. They all know exactly where they are when they are on the water and would never mistake a lighthouse for an oncoming ship.

But this story illustrates the point very nicely. It is common for humans to assume that we know everything that we need to know to make the decisions we make. It is even more common for us to make up our minds and shout out our intentions without having all the facts.

After we have made up our minds and made a decision we regret it is too late to ask for guidance. At that point, we are only doing damage control. Proverbs 16:18 speaks to us across the centuries and reminds us that *Pride goes before destruction a haughty spirit before a fall NIV*

When To Identify Your Lighthouse

We need wisdom beyond our own at so many of life's crucial junctures. Without it we are prone to make errors that can cost us years of happiness. So the best time to find a lighthouse is before you crash on the rocks. If you wait too late to find the lighthouse you are spending time repairing instead of preparing. It really is easier to prepare than to repair, and a lighthouse in your life can help with that.

Once you have a situation in which you need advice and you don't know anyone that can help, the best thing to do is to ask. You can ask your pastor or your boss, your banker, the principal at your child's school, or any number of respected people in your community. Consider what type of advice you need and find someone you know who knows about that. Most professionals are very happy to set aside some time to give counsel to someone who approaches them with a request for advice. Just ask. That is the starting point. Recognize that when you need counsel you should ask for it. Ask before you make any decisions that are irrevocable.

Living Near the Lighthouse

There is another, more life-giving way to have a lighthouse in your life, and that is to simply spend time associating with those you admire. Make friends with people who have the wisdom or skills that you would like to have. This circle of friends can serve as lighthouses just by being present in the harbor. Observe how they live. Notice how they talk and what they talk about. Watch them as they develop their spirits and their minds.

As you are building relationships remember that we are highly influenced by the people we spend the most time with. Allow the maturity and wisdom of others to shape you and help you develop more wisdom and maturity. Listen, watch and learn. This is how all of us become stronger and better: we emulate those who are stronger and wiser than we ourselves are right now.

Accept that to grow, we must change and that change can be uncomfortable. Be willing to be uncomfortable for a time to become more like the lighthouse. No one is born knowing all that they need to know. We are all learning every moment of our lives, and it is up to each individual to make use of the education that we receive through experience, observation and listening. In this way, we can avoid the worst of life-changing disasters, such as substance abuse, overspending, or neglecting our relationships.

So let me reiterate here that it is a good idea to have some lighthouses identified in your community before a real need for them is upon you. To have a lighthouse, you know that you can trust it is important to know what qualities and characteristics to look for.

Identify Your Lighthouses

The ability to mentor or offer wise counsel is not a gift that everyone possesses. It takes maturity and wisdom. These two qualities are found in many people; you just have to recognize and respect it when you find it. But be watchful: People who are smart are not necessarily wise, and people who are old are not necessarily mature. Here is a short definition of both of these traits:

Wisdom is knowledge that has aged like fine wine or a rare violin. Wisdom is knowing how to use the information at hand. Maturity is being able to do what must be done even when you don't want to do it. Maturity is being able to set aside what you want in order for someone you love to have what they need.

Being a lighthouse also takes awareness, compassion, and tact. A lighthouse can speak the truth in love. It requires the ability to think before speaking and a willingness to consider more than one side of any issue. Every situation has more than one facet and a strong mentor knows this.

In addition to having these character traits, your lighthouse may need expertise in the area you need advice in. If it is specialized, such as finances or building an addition to the house, this is particularly crucial. As a rule, you can use the following guidelines for choosing a lighthouse for your Harbor Home.

A Lighthouse is Selfless

A lighthouse is able to walk in your shoes. A good lighthouse has a strong sense of what others are experiencing. They are empathetic and therefore they don't make your issue about themselves. They are able to stop thinking about themselves long enough to tune in to you and hear what you are saying.

Your lighthouse will listen well and attentively. This is possibly the rarest of selfless acts. Most people listen just long enough to formulate a response or an argument rather than listening to understand. Your lighthouse should be able to hear you and what is in your heart because they listen to understand. This really means that they know how to ask good questions and they hear what you are not saying as much as what you are saying.

A Lighthouse is Mature

I like the five-year-plus guideline. In general, and for matters that are spiritual or deeply personal, I seek someone that is at least five years older than I am. This person will probably be enough ahead of me on life's journey to have seen and experienced things that I haven't. They have had the opportunity to grow and learn for five years longer than I have, and that often has some advantages.

Their children may be five years older than mine, their marriage may be five years more mature than mine and they may have walked with the Lord five years longer than I. You can see the advantage of a bit more maturity and insight. The five-year-plus guideline is just that: a guideline. What you are really looking for is maturity. Unless it's a technology question. Then find the nearest ten-year-old. Fast.

A Lighthouse Has Been There and Done That (Successfully)

If you have been a stepmother for a short time and you are hitting all the snags and hiccups that are part of that role, you need to find another stepmother who has not only been a stepmother longer than you have but has successfully overcome some of the issues you are facing. In this example, a stepmother whose stepchildren are grown and have come to respect and love her as a friend is your best choice. She has had some time to gain perspective, to look back with a bit of objectivity on her own mistakes and what she would do differently given a chance.

No matter what you want or need help thinking through you can probably find someone who has done it or something similar well. Step-parenting, welding, designing a backyard patio, growing herbs, toilet training your child, vegan cooking, having a better attitude toward your boss, loving your spouse; in all these things you can seek help and there is no shame in it. But find someone who knows how and has demonstrated true skill.

A Lighthouse or a Friend

A lighthouse is there to light your way, not share your darkness. When you need encouragement or support or if you need to know that other people are the same kind of crazy as you, go talk to a friend who is on the same path at the same place as you are. Vent. Talk it out. Ask if they are okay. Be honest if you are not okay. A true friend will listen. Encourage one another. Pray about it together. But don't try to be a lighthouse for one another. Jesus taught us that blind guides lead one another into a pit (Matthew 15:14).

Be careful of asking for advice that your friend doesn't have the insight to offer. And here's another thing: don't offer advice that you don't have the insight to offer. You can share an example of what you did to get through a moment, but if you are still struggling in an area and you are just as lost as your friend, say that. Be honest. It is okay if you don't have all the answers to your friend's problem or your own. That is why God gives us lighthouses. If you need guidance, find a lighthouse. Introduce them to your friend. Then go talk it out.

A Lighthouse is Dependable

A lighthouse is one of those people who are "always there". You know the ones I mean. They respond to your texts, answer their phones, reply to emails, meet you for coffee when they say they will, and arrive on time. Lighthouses stay in the action when others go MIA. A lighthouse never sends your call straight through to voicemail.

It is an eternal truth that you know which of your friends you can count on by what they do when you are a hot mess. Those who turn and run when you are going through a divorce, or your child has been diagnosed with leukemia, or the company you work for closes with no notice are not serving as a lighthouse in your life.

Trust the ones who continue to walk the path with you when the path is rocky and narrow. Those may very well be your lighthouses. Cherish them. Ask them for a steady light for your path back to the harbor. A lighthouse can't keep itself from shining, and it will help light your way. They can't walk the way for you, but they can put a light on the path.

It is during a major life crisis such as divorce, unemployment, chronic illness or injury, and other life-changing events that you will get some big surprises about who your lighthouses are. You may think that you know who will be there with you as you go through the worst days of your life but you could very well be wrong.

You might be startled by the people who stand by your side through it all. It could be that someone you only know casually will be the one to step up and be the bright lighthouse that offers the most wisdom, support, and encouragement as you stumble through the dark. These amazing people are a blessing that you will never forget.

Occasionally, as difficult as this may seem, you will count on someone to be a lighthouse and they will not fill that role for you. If you discover this when you need them most, it can be a devastating discovery. It can feel as though you have been wounded twice. Once by the situation you are in and then by what feels like a friends' betrayal.

Be aware that not everyone who has the ability to be a lighthouse has the strength to be a lighthouse. It is very hard to stand firm with someone you love when they are deeply hurt and in need of a loving guide. It could be that your closest friends and family cannot bear the pain of seeing you in distress.

In the midst of your crisis, the one you counted on to be a light for you may be in a situation that you are not aware of. Perhaps they are simply too exhausted by their own life circumstances to shine a light for you. Judge them gently. The Lord will send you a lighthouse, and it will be who you need.

A Lighthouse is a Bright Light

When you are in darkness, you need a light. Lighthouses offer hope and dispel the gloom. Lighthouses create light, not shadows. Your lighthouses should bring a ray of hope to you. They should remind you that even on the worst day of your life there will be a time when it will be a memory and a survival story.

You will get through it. Whatever it is. This is the repeated message of a lighthouse. You can do it. You are loved. You are a child of God. A lighthouse carries the message that everything will be okay in the end, and if everything is not okay then we are not yet at the end.

Lighthouses encourage you to keep going. Get with it. Find a way to make a way. Give God room to make a way. But you do your part too. They let you cry but they don't let you keep crying when it is time to get moving again. Lighthouses point out that there is light in the darkest moments and you will be through this soon.

If your lighthouse is dragging you into the darkness by pointing out how bad your circumstances are without offering suggestions for lighting a way through it, find another lighthouse. In true physical darkness, the human eye can see a single candle flame at least as far away as three miles, perhaps further according to some studies. In true spiritual darkness, a human heart can sense the light of encouragement across all eternity. Be a light to others and if your light grows dim or goes out, find a lighthouse that will set you to glowing again. A true lighthouse will do this.

Being a Lighthouse

Make no mistake: everyone has a gift and a contribution to make and everyone has something to offer. If they are two or ninety-two, everyone can contribute to the collective wisdom of the harbor. No single, authoritarian individual is the possessor of all knowledge. In your Harbor Home, everyone gets a chance to shine.

Because of this truth, not every lighthouse in our family is older and wiser; the seven-year-old who reminds the four-year-old not to go outside until an adult is with them is acting as a lighthouse and guide. The ten-year-old who can make the printer send a fax is a guide at that moment. It is important to praise these steps toward becoming a lighthouse.

We know a family whose seven-year-old has an astounding gift of putting together jigsaw puzzles. During the time when most children attended school virtually, his school had a virtual talent show. This little guy's family encouraged him to shine his light and demonstrate his ability to put together puzzles for this talent show. How this worked I have no idea, but the point is that he won third place and the respect of his peers. He is a lighthouse to those of us who really can't do those things.

The importance of allowing a child to lead in their area of giftedness is hard to overstate. You are setting an example of working together and taking sound advice. Being able to receive good advice is a skill worth developing. Remember that we resist receiving advice. Help your child get ahead of this very human flaw. Teach them how to learn by learning from their teaching.

Observe your children and notice what they know how to do well. Comment on those things. Praise their abilities. Make meaningful observations. Ask them to show you how to do the things that they know how to do. Allow yourself to learn from them. This builds their confidence, helps them learn how to organize their thoughts and consider how they do what they do. It also helps them learn how to communicate more clearly.

The little things that your child can do are going to be simple, age-appropriate activities. A three-year-old learning how to stack blocks and create a bridge can show you how it is done. Ask them to tell you how this is accomplished. Ask permission to try it too. Then you build alongside them. A five-year-old making a peanut butter and jelly sandwich can teach you the fine points of creating this delicacy. A ten-year-old drawing pictures of airplanes will be happy to show you how. Help them become a guide.

Being a lighthouse doesn't have to mean that you have the answer to all things. A couple of years ago I needed a lighthouse that could walk me through the secrets of making a decent meringue for a pie. I found that lighthouse in my ninety-year-old mother-in-law who couldn't remember what day of the week it was. But she absolutely remembered how to make meringue. Anyone can be a lighthouse, and it is a truly generous and loving act to let the people around you shine.

As you reach out as a lighthouse to others, go back and read again what qualities a lighthouse possesses. Cultivate these in yourself. Before you claim the place of honor as a lighthouse in someone else's life make sure that you have the skills and qualities. Develop these skills so that when someone needs you are ready to serve with gladness and competence.

Summary of Chapter Four

Are there harbor lights and lighthouses in your life? Who guides you back to safety when you are lost at sea? Seek them out and let them guide you by example.

Don't let pride stand in the way of seeking a guide that can help you create a Harbor Home. Overcoming the pride that prevents us from reaching out for the help that we need is as simple as saying, "I need advice." Practice saying that right now. Aloud. Where you are. Just say it. If you say it once, you will see that it is not fatal, and you will be able to say it again and again.

Help your children and others learn how to be a lighthouse by giving them opportunities to guide you in areas where they shine. This helps your children gain confidence and lets you model the skill of learning.

Your Harbor Home needs at least one steady light shining reliably through the foggy mornings and dark, moonless nights. Find your lighthouse and walk up the sidewalk to visit. We all love lighthouses, and you know what else? Lighthouses love us back.

Questions for Discussion or Deeper Thinking

1. Describe a time when someone gave you solid advice or guidance. How was your life changed by this?
2. Write down an example of how you can ask for guidance when you need it. How can you overcome the pride that keeps you from asking?
3. Who can you identify right now that you trust to be your lighthouse?
4. Make a list of the lighthouse qualities you already possess. Which can you begin to develop?
5. Determine some areas in which other members of your household really shine. How can you encourage them to share their gifts?

Chapter Five

HARBOR MASTERS, CAPTAINS, AND MATES: ROLES, RULES, ROUTINES

For there is no authority except what God has established.
Romans 13:1

The public dock of Ocracoke Harbor is maintained by the United States National Parks Service. The dock itself is a simple concrete walkway that serves as a sidewalk near the ferry docks on the village end of the island. Cyclists and pedestrians use it, but they have to dodge the power outlets and cleats that are there for the boats.

There are facilities there for pleasure boaters to come and tie up to the dock and, for a small fee, stay overnight and enjoy being part of the village life. Shops, restaurants, hotels, and other amenities are within easy walking distance, and many boaters traveling up or down the eastern seaboard take advantage of this picturesque stop.

The road that goes around this part of the cove of this harbor looks a little like an anthill during the tourist season. People are in and out of boats, getting ready to go on fishing expeditions or coming back from one, carrying goods and products into and out of the shops and restaurants and other work-a-day activities.

There are boat tours of the area available during which you could see dolphins, flying fish and the beautiful coast. There are vendors renting bicycles and motor scooters, kayaks, and stand-up paddleboards. There are a couple of snow cone stands and lots of people. It is a laid-back and friendly place with a great many moving parts.

Whenever I walk through this very busy part of the village along the dock there are a couple of signs that always catch my eye. Written on them in clearly printed, succinctly stated language are the rules and expectations for when your personal boat is docked here. These rules are pretty basic and seem to be, in the main, followed by all. The signs are posted at eye level so no one can miss them and no one has to guess what the rules are. Having these rules in place makes life at Silver Lake Harbor, Ocracoke Island more comfortable for everyone. Boundaries are good.

Rules and expectations are essential for community life. They help us to remember that we do not live in our harbor alone. We share the space with others who matter to us. They are not meant to restrict us in a punitive manner but, instead, rules are there to serve as guardrails to help ensure the wellbeing of everyone. Every Harbor Home needs boundaries that regulate the flow of life within it, as well as someone whose role it is to keep the rules clear, visible, and enforced.

There are also clearly marked roles that are noted on various signs. You will notice commercial fishing vessels with the name of the captain written on a placard near its berth in the harbor. There may also be a notation made of the names of the mates that serve on board. There is another sign that indicates the office in which the dock master, or harbormaster, works. In a busy working harbor like your home, there is enough that needs to be done to keep everyone busy and involved in keeping the harbor working.

In this chapter, we will be diving into how we can create within our homes appropriate roles, rules, and routines that will unify our families and help us to see that we, as a family, share more than just a place to sleep, shower and do laundry. Order begins with some decisions that are in place for the comfort and benefit of everyone.

Chapter Five will be dedicated to how those decisions can be made, how and why you can select the rules that regulate your harbor, and the roles that we all play in maintaining the expectations. These three things work together to keep our families safe and remind us that we are all accountable to each other.

Families are designed to love each other. Every human being no matter their cultural background, their socio-economic level, or the amount of education they have, wants to live in a harbor home that is safe, harmonious, and happy. As adults, we need to make sure that the rules are appropriate for the situation and that they are enforced reasonably and appropriately. We also need to make sure that there is a role for everyone and that the routines of our lives help us to live well. Let's begin by looking at some roles in the harbor.

Roles

The Harbormaster

In commercial or large municipal marinas, there is an individual whose title is harbormaster. A harbormaster is an official who is responsible for enforcing the regulations of a particular harbor to promote safe navigation and security in the harbor. A harbormaster watches over the harbor with an experienced and well-trained eye.

This individual can tell when something is wrong or when someone is not safe and needs help. They understand their harbor and know it like the back of their hand. It is a position held only by well-seasoned, mature mariners. This role is well respected within the harbor, and the decisions made by the harbormaster are firm.

Because of this, the harbormaster makes decisions carefully and without the motivations of holding power, having personal comfort or out of a sense of greed. The harbormaster strives to be correct and mature because he or she is in charge of keeping the lives and property of everyone in the harbor safe. Selfish, egotistic, hot-tempered harbormasters are far less successful and receive far less respect from the community than those who know that their job is to protect and have stewardship over the harbor. Harbormasters are careful about what they tell others to do because they know that others will do what is asked, and if the harbormaster gets it wrong, the entire harbor is wrong too.

In your Harbor Home, the harbormaster is probably the mother or the father. Certainly, the harbormaster is an adult with some experience as well as responsibility for the care of the family. There are many ways to be a good parent or head of household. Everyone makes this role their own. God gave you your children and the instincts to protect and nurture them. You love your children and want to raise them to be successful, secure, and happy. Each and every parent around the world want this for their children.

Every parent also has their own parenting style. Experts in family psychology have determined that there are four general classifications into which every parent falls and this represents their overall parenting guidelines. The four classifications are:

- Authoritarian or Disciplinarian
- Permissive or Indulgent
- Uninvolved
- Authoritative

Authoritarian or disciplinarian parenting is mostly known for having the rules established by one all-powerful authority figure in the home and unquestioning obedience by all other members of the family is expected.

Permissive or indulgent parenting has very few rules or expectations, and those rules are pretty flexible. Mostly the parent allows the children to set their own agenda and provides care and nurture along with minimal instruction.

Uninvolved parenting is what it sounds like. In homes with uninvolved parents, the parents provide little in the way of care, nurture, structure, or instruction, and the children meet their own needs the best that they can. These parents love their children deeply, but do not involve themselves in raising their children beyond very basic levels of care.

Authoritative parenting is characterized by the parents in the home presenting a strong authority figure. Additionally, the rules in the home are based on the needs of the family. The rules can be flexible as those needs change and exceptions may be granted after some discussion. Homes in which the parents are authoritative have structure and instruction as well as well-organized and predictable patterns of behavior.

These descriptions are highly generalized and are here so that you can do more research if you desire, but you can probably recognize which of these four categories you fit in. You may also be able to identify the kind of parenting that you were raised with. If you are interested in learning more details about each style there is a lot of information available. Knowing more about your parenting style could help you understand a little more about yourself and why you respond to parenting as you do.

As the harbormaster, you can choose to function in a different category if you are not comfortable with the one in which you parent now. If you were raised by parents who parented in one style and you would rather parent differently, you can make that choice. You are not stuck with what your parents chose. More importantly, you are not stuck with what you have chosen up until now. Being intentional about choosing your parenting style is part of being a good harbormaster.

How you choose to operate your Harbor Home and how you choose to be the harbormaster is very personal and there are many factors that will guide your decisions. These factors may include any special needs that your children may have, any health problems that you or another family member may be experiencing, the demands placed on you from your place of work or any of several other factors. There is absolutely no one correct way to be a parent or to run your home.

In general, however, the authoritative parenting style is considered to provide children with the most stable and secure home life. When parents are making decisions about rules and behavior expectations, while keeping in mind the needs and the temperaments of all the family members, there is a sense that the rules are there to protect rather than punish. When parents take an authoritative approach, their home is more likely to be harmonious and unified. You can take this approach within your own personality and the specific structure of your family.

The harbormaster is watchful and careful and understands how important this role is. It is this one who is ultimately responsible for the entire harbor. This person has earned the right to be in charge because they have a proven track record of being aware of the needs of everyone in the harbor and the ability to meet those needs. The harbormaster cares for others above themselves. They consider this role to be a sacred trust and know that the quality of life for everyone hinges to a large degree on how well the harbor is cared for.

What this means for your family is that the mother and/or father are in the primary position of making sure that the family is running well and they are willing to consistently make personal sacrifices for the overall good of their family. This goes beyond loving their family. It means meeting the needs of others before meeting their own needs. The best harbormasters know that love all by itself is not enough.

The harbormaster can and should delegate responsibilities to others that have the aptitude and maturity to take them on. For example, the harbormaster makes sure that the trash gets taken out but does not necessarily take it out personally. Parceling out chores is part of good organization. Being in charge is not easy. It is not giving a constant stream of orders. Neither does the harbormaster do everything while the others in the harbor sit and dangle their feet in the water. The harbormaster encourages, instructs, coaches, supports, inspires, and pushes. And works. The harbormaster is in constant communication with the next group we are going to discuss: the captains.

Captains

Every boat has a captain. Usually, you can identify them because they are the one who is driving the boat. A captain's license is necessary for carrying passengers commercially but, as a rule, the one who is driving any boat from the smallest kayak to the largest cabin cruiser or sailboat is considered to be the captain.

The captain is in charge of the safe operation of their own ship. He or she knows how to run the ship and can steer it reliably from place to place. The captain is aware and competent, trustworthy, and reliable and is willing to take responsibility for navigating the ship safely. This is a position that requires skill and dependability.

In your Harbor Home, the individual in the role of captain may change over time or due to special circumstances. There may also be a few captains over the various areas of responsibility. Captains have jurisdiction over one area, and you know that your harbor home has many areas that need care.

For example, your six-year-old can be the captain of his own room. You as the harbormaster have standards for how each room is to be kept, but it is up to the captain to maintain this. He may need to be taught how to tidy his room (many times) but he is the captain and therefore is in charge of meeting the harbormaster's expectations.

He may also be the captain of feeding the pets. Your captains will probably have more than one ship to manage especially as they get older. They may be in charge of their own school work and their part-time job and being strong members of their baseball teams. With maturity, children can take on more responsibility.

When someone is a captain in charge of an area, that area is their ship to operate. In order for them to be functioning well in the harbor, they must understand that their area is vital. The harbormaster instructs the captains concerning the rules and expectations of the harbor and then respects and praises the captain for managing their ship. Strong captains make the harbor strong, but strong harbormasters make strong captains. Make sure that you are affirming work that is done well.

In working harbors, just like in your home, most people wear more than one hat. So the harbormaster is almost certainly also a captain. In your home, you may, by necessity, be the captain of transportation or meal preparation or laundry as well as being the harbormaster that coordinates all other areas. Life in your harbor home is busy and full, but it is also totally manageable.

Captains and harbormasters also have another important job. In fact, I think this is the most important job they have. Captains and harbormasters are responsible for training the mates. It is impossible to overstate how crucial this is. Training others to be able to run the harbor means that the harbor is more stable. The more people in your home who are capable of keeping it running smoothly the more secure everyone is. Let's discuss for a few minutes those marvelous mates.

Mates

Mates are those wonderful and necessary ones who are learning and helping and undergirding the work of the harbor most often by doing chores that require a low level of skill and a high level of willingness. They have not yet become captains of the area in which they are working, but they are essential to healthy function.

As with the role of captain, the role of a mate can be taken up by the harbormaster or it can be taken up by a captain. Remember that roles in your home are assigned to the people best suited to fill them. And sometimes the person most suited to be a captain is usually a mate. Now, someone who is accustomed to being the captain may find it challenging to be thrust into the mate position, but roles go to the one most able to successfully fill it, and, in a harbor home, we work together.

One of the traits of strong leaders is that they know what they don't know and they are able to say that when they don't know something. They are also able to recognize when someone else may be better able to take charge of a situation. But a truly wonderful trait is when a leader is willing to learn from someone who is typically in a subordinate role to them. That is excellence in leadership and is seldom found.

A great example of this is when you are on your smartphone and one of the children knows how to do something with that phone that you don't. You have three options when this happens:

- You can tell your child that you don't want them messing with your phone.
- You can hand the phone to the child and ask them to do for you whatever it is that you need to do. Or . . .
- You can ask them to teach you how to do whatever it is.

If you want to elevate your child even more you can ask if they can show you anything else, after they have shown you how to fix your more urgent problem. Be their mate and let them be the captain for that moment. It is a valuable lesson.

Here is an important note for captains and harbormasters who are training mates: when you are training them, it is not so that they can be your helpers. You must train them so that they can be your replacements. The goal of training the people of your harbor is for them to be able to run the harbor without you. Remember that you are raising your children to be independent and successful in their own right.

Mates are not supposed to remain mates forever. They are, from the very beginning, supposed to be raised to become captains and harbormasters who will contribute to their community and, ultimately, to all of society.

Treat and teach these future captains with strength and clarity but also with respect and grace. Remember that you were once a mate, and teach them the way you wanted to be taught. Remember to be the mate whenever you can and give others the opportunity to be the captain.

When my son was eleven years old or thereabouts we had a fax machine in our home. This would have been in the early to mid-1990s. It was a new technology to have in a home even though there had been larger office models available for a while. They were strange and foreign devices to me, and I had been given this to facilitate a volunteer role I had taken on in our region.

I had been given, along with the machine itself, an instruction manual and a tutorial. Neither seemed to do me much good. To me, this gadget looked like a telephone that had put on a lot of weight. The paper came in rolls that had to be placed just exactly right in the receptacle, and the paper itself was shiny and felt slimy to the touch. This thing was supposed to help us communicate, but I was having a very hard time learning how to use it.

The day came when it rang for the first time and gave a signal that someone was sending me a fax. I just stared at it. My son came into the room to watch this cool new thing do what it was supposed to do. Unbeknownst to me, he had read the instruction manual and had walked himself through a tutorial. So while I stood there with my mouth hanging open and my heart pounding he told me that I had to pick up the receiver. I looked at him with wild eyes and told him that I didn't know what to do.

He looked over at me and shook his head in amazement. Then he stepped up to the machine and received the fax like he had been doing it for years. He walked out of the room still shaking his head. As he passed me he patted me on the shoulder (he had just gotten tall enough to do that) and said, "Mom, what would you do without me?"

My answer was that I had no idea, but at the very least he was going to have to teach me (again) how to work that thing. I finally did learn but not until fax machines were practically obsolete and were being replaced in the home with other technology. At that moment, he was the captain and I was an incompetent mate. We both learned a lot about roles that day. And his innocent question, "Mom, what would you do without me?" still causes a catch in my throat. Just like it did that day.

Roles are important because they help us to avoid confusion and function more efficiently and effectively. Roles are not designed to limit an individual but to help them understand how to grow and be involved in the community. Roles are assigned or sometimes they are taken up voluntarily, but they are not meant to be permanent. The captain today may be a mate tomorrow. Today's mate will become the harbormaster sooner than we dare to believe.

A sign that you are an excellent captain is that you know when you should step aside and let someone else be the captain. Let others in your harbor home shine. Give them organic opportunities to practice being a leader and let them learn from your example how to be a mate. Remember: you are not training your helpers, you are training your replacements.

Rules

Rules are very often misinterpreted as restrictive edicts sent down from an autocratic being bent on destroying all the fun. This perception is particularly true among younger or less mature members of the community. Rules, in truth, are meant to protect those who might endanger themselves or others by engaging in behavior that seems like fun, but in reality, is dangerous or disruptive. Rules are not fences, they are guardrails.

Another frequent perception about rules is that they are not always fair. This perception, unlike the other, is often true. It is entirely true and completely appropriate that rules are, very often, not what many young people would call fair. When you are the adult in charge there are a great many times when you will be called upon to explain that rules do not always seem fair, but they are still in place.

Rules are not fair because they change over time and with the maturity and capability of each individual. If your harbor home consists of an early elementary-aged person, a teenager, and two adults then the rules that apply to one don't necessarily apply to the others. In our home, no one was allowed to eat on the couch until they were fifteen years old. This kept the upholstery a bit cleaner. Of course, this seems a terrible injustice to the fourteen-year-old who thinks they are capable of snacking neatly.

Rules are not fair, but that is okay. They are not meant to be fair, they are meant to keep us safe and working well together. Because of this and because we must live and work together, we comply with rules that we don't like, rules that we don't understand, and rules that we disagree with. Even if they don't seem fair.

Some of the most challenging concepts for children learning to live in a community whether it be a family or classroom or other group setting concern rules of behavior. Things that we can do or cannot do, things that we can say or cannot say, schedules, timing, where we can go, and how fast we get there.

Some children are more compliant and are actually very glad that there are boundaries for community behavior. My first-born, a beautiful daughter, was such a child. I once overheard her saying to one of my friends that breaking the rules made her feel tense. Let me say that now, thirty years later, nothing has changed about that. She remains a follower of the rules and has been very successful.

Other children are more apt to challenge the rules. These children can try your patience and test your endurance, but they have a great many natural attributes that, when properly channeled, help them become successful and visionary adults.

These children can be very creative as they look for ways to actively break the rules. They busily look for loopholes or exceptions, while the more compliant children generally accept the collective wisdom of the community that sets the rules. They seem to understand that rules have a purpose and a reason for being there. Dealing with these two types requires two very different approaches.

Tips For Leading Compliant Children

First, I encourage you to resist the temptation to place expectations on this child that you don't place on your less compliant child just because you know that they will do what you ask. It is easy to ask the same child over and over to take out the garbage when you know that that child will simply do it while the other child will argue or complain. Make sure that you ask everyone to do their share regardless of temperament.

Secondly, it is important to think carefully and be cautious about what you ask of these children. As a rule, they will do what you expect them to do. Many years ago when my children were young and we were homeschooling, my daughter asked if she could go to public school. She knew many girls in public school from her church group and her scout troop and other places, and she wanted to go. I had deep reservations.

I was familiar with the school that she would have to attend and, in those days, we had no way to choose a different school. I wanted her to be happy and to enjoy her early adolescent years. I knew that she was very social and I was concerned that, in spite of my genuine efforts to keep her busy and active with friends, she was still lonely. But the middle school was truly substandard. I wanted her to be well educated.

I honestly didn't know what to do. My biggest concern in that moment was that I knew that whatever I decided she would comply with a good attitude. I knew that she wouldn't push back.

Whatever I said she would do. She wouldn't tell me I was wrong or refuse to cooperate or pout or cry or anything. I had to figure out and do what was right for her. It required a great deal of thought and prayer.

In the end, I asked her to remain at home until she could enter high school. It was a better school with more strong academic choices, and I had several friends on the faculty who respected and cared for her. She seemed satisfied with that and I continued to arrange for as many larger group activities as possible.

I still do not know if I did the right thing but she has a master's degree and some graduate certificates and she is highly successful in a satisfying career and she is happy. She has an enormous friend circle and a lovely family. It seems to have worked out. Whew. The point is, be careful about your decisions in regards to a compliant child.

Do not misunderstand compliant children. They want to push back against rules that they don't like but they don't want to risk any consequences. They are more careful about how and when they push back.

These children require as much vigilance as the less compliant children in your life because they can be sneaky about breaking rules and we typically are less likely to suspect them when something happens like the cat being tossed down the laundry chute.

Compliant children also are very aware that if something happens and the culprit is not easily identified, they are not likely to be suspected. Yet they will seldom speak up when their sibling or classmate is unfairly accused of the misdeed. Be aware. These sweet, easy children can be tricky.

Of course, the less compliant child will have challenges of a different kind. These little darlings will be sure to let you know when a rule or requirement does not suit them. It would be easy to remain in a constant state of combat with them. But there is another way. The child who could argue with a brick wall can learn how to cooperate.

Tips For Leading Less Compliant Children

Keeping your voice well-modulated is important in every harbor home but when you have a child who consistently pushes back against your reasonable expectations it is even more so. Shouting even when you are frustrated is counterproductive and is an indicator that you have lost control of the situation. When there is conflict between parties look to see who is shouting and you will know who is not in charge. So, resist the urge to shout.

Rather than shouting, lower the volume of your voice. This requires your child to listen to hear you and gives them the reassuring sense that you are still in charge. Remember that even though this child may behave as though they want to be in charge, they do not. They really want to know that they are safe and that you are at the helm. Let them know that you are in charge by keeping your voice down.

When you ask your child to be in compliance with the expectations of the home or do a task such as schoolwork, pet care, or something and they push back or delay, there are some measured responses that you can use to help.

The first tip is to consider prior to requiring that a chore be done if it can wait a few minutes. A non-compliant child may be more successful if they are given a heads up. For example, the trash needs to go out. You can tell your child that in five minutes the trash must go out and that you have set the timer.

Set the timer and when the signal sounds, wait a moment for your child to respond. If they do not take the trash out, tell them that the timer has sounded and that you expect them to do what they were asked. Keep your voice low and firm. If this tactic doesn't work the first time. Keep trying. Stay calm.

This can work because the timer becomes the voice of authority and the child has a sense of control. I am not a psychologist, but I have noticed that non-compliant children often seem to need to have a sense of more control over their own lives. They sometimes seem to me to be more anxious and mistrustful than their compliant peers. Have some grace with these children while helping them become cooperative members of your harbor home. They may have anxiety that is showing out as non-compliance.

The "do it first" technique is another good way to remind your child that rules are generally not optional. Let's revisit the trash situation. If you ask your child to take out the trash and the response is a protest or argument you can firmly and calmly tell your child that you will be glad to discuss this with them but that first, they must do what they were told. In other words, we will talk about your feelings about taking out the trash after you have taken out the trash. Do it first, then we will talk.

If, after they take out the trash, they still want to talk about it, listen to them. Hear them out. If they feel that their sibling "never" takes out the trash while they themselves "always" take out the trash, suggest that they draw up a tally sheet and keep tabs for a few days.

For clarity, let me reiterate that the child makes the tally sheet and keeps up with it. Not you. Be creative. Have the child solve their own problem. It is not helpful for you to solve all the issues. Your child can learn to think through to the logical conclusion that it is just taking the trash out. It's not that big a deal.

Another technique is to demonstrate how much time is wasted arguing. Let's go back to the trash. You ask your child to take out the trash and the pushback begins. Look at your watch or a clock and be obvious about it. Note the time out loud. For example, say aloud that it is now 3:47 pm. Then remind them that if they simply take the trash out they can go back to doing whatever they were doing by 3:52. If instead, they want to spend that time discussing it, they will not get back to what they were doing until 4:00. Whichever option they choose, the trash must still go out.

Assure them that they will still have to take the trash out and that they are only wasting their own time. This puts the consequences of their actions squarely on their own shoulders. The secret to making this work is remaining calm and assuring your child that how they want to spend their spare time is entirely up to them but that if it were you, you would just take out the trash and get it done.

Non-verbal cues are very helpful with less compliant children. Timers, alarms set on phones, or automated reminders generated by a computer calendar can all help keep your less compliant child on track. This will lessen the conflict and arguing significantly. Especially with consistent use over time.

These are just a few techniques that worked for me. You are the one who knows your child best and you will be able to help them gain a steady foothold in your home better than anyone else. Bear in mind that shouting, insulting, and issuing idle threats are not effective under any circumstances. You can do this.

None of these techniques will work if you do not work to keep them in place. Consistency is the key to all routines and habits. If you show me a child that gets up and takes out the trash the first time he is asked, I will show you a mother that consistently worked a plan to make that happen. It all starts with the harbormaster.

One more point before we leave the subject of non-compliant children: they are not always the guilty party. The very active non-compliant child is not the only one who might break or spill something. It is easy to place blame on the child that always seems to be into something or doing something that they shouldn't be. That doesn't mean that they are always the one who did it this time. Justice in the home is important.

In homes and classrooms, there is almost always one or maybe two convenient scapegoats for all disruptions. Consistently blaming the same child will damage that child if they are indeed innocent. They may decide that since they are going to be blamed anyway they might as well act out. As an adult, it is your job to make sure that you know you are right when you place blame or consequences on a child. If you didn't see the incident with your own eyes, be careful when you make an accusation.

I know that all of these techniques take up time and patience and energy. You may be strongly tempted to yell or scold or blow up, but try to stay the course. Children who are developing as expected can learn to live in cooperation with their family no matter what their temperament is.

Tips on Consequences For Any Temperament

As a rule, I discourage spanking because it is so easy for it to get out of hand and become the only consequence that a parent uses. I know that there is Biblical justification for spanking children and there are times, when a child is still young, (under eight years of age) that it can be effectively used as instant negative feedback.

There are other consequences that work just as well to help you teach your child your expectations without running the risk of damaging your relationship with them. This is a personal decision but I urge you to be cautious and to make sure that you are not just venting your frustration on a child that is still learning.

Parents who overuse spanking are setting their children up for childhood and adolescent depression and are also very likely to find that their relationship with their children, even as the decades pass, is not what they hoped. This can easily escalate into abuse and that is unacceptable. A quick swat on the rear is usually a sufficient and instant reminder. Once your children are eight, you need to be more creative.

Another rule of thumb is to remember that every child, including adolescent children, has an attention span that is pretty short. Telling a child that they are "grounded" for a month or six months or a year is ridiculous, pointless, and ineffective.

Removing privileges is an effective consequence when behavior is unacceptable, but the timeline must have a limit that children can track. After a few days with privileges removed a child doesn't really remember the action that created the loss. It is possible that you don't either. To make this consequence meaningful, they have to remember what they lost and why. When they get it back, they are glad to try again.

Experiencing consequences that are logical and occur naturally is the best way for any of us to learn. One Sunday afternoon in late autumn we had a family fishing outing at a friend's home on the lake. After nearly everyone had gone home one young mother and her small son remained behind to help clean up. They were on the dock straightening chairs when the little boy mentioned that he had not gotten to swim that day.

His mother explained to him that none of us had gone swimming because the water had turned cold. He was less than impressed with this explanation. It is important at this point in the story to tell you that this little boy was still wearing the life jacket that he and all the children were required to wear all afternoon. Well, you guessed it, the little guy jumped right in the water and I could hear him gasp as the cold water hit him.

I watched in admiration as the mother calmly reminded him that she had told him the water was cold. She did not shout, berate him, or panic. She helped him get out of the water and then finished what she was doing. He was cold while he waited to go home and, his mom told me later, he was cold in the car every mile of the way home. Legend has it that he never jumped into a cold lake again. Natural consequences.

Whenever you can, allow your children to learn from their mistakes by simply letting things take their natural course. A favorite toy left behind at a friend's house doesn't have to be fetched by the parent immediately. Waiting until the next visit for the toy to be available can be a helpful reminder for your child to make sure they have everything they need before going anywhere.

Of course, there are times when learning this way is dangerous or impractical. Aren't you glad that you didn't have to get hit by a car to learn to look before crossing the street? Sometimes the only way for your children to learn the things they need to know is for you to teach them. But how you teach determines how well they learn.

Every mistake your child makes, every time they get something wrong, or they defy you or have a bad attitude is an opportunity for you to love them even more. The child that challenges authority needs a lot of attention, time, love, and patience. Correction is an important part of educating your children; a firm and patient hand is key.

The role of a parent is primarily a teaching role. First and foremost you are your child's teacher. Their first teacher. Their best teacher. The teacher who will teach them more about living and loving and being an adult than all their other teachers combined. This is a holy mission and one for which God created you specifically.

Routines

Several years ago I found in a thrift shop a book on how to be a good mother that was written in the early 1950s. The illustrations were a fun look at historic fashion. The women in the pictures wore shirtwaist dresses with flared skirts. They accessorized these dresses with dainty flat shoes and faux pearl necklaces. The content was pretty interesting and definitely dated. More than that it spoke volumes about the era in which the book was written.

The book, lost after several moves, was filled with tips about sterilizing glass bottles and nipples, laundering cloth diapers and baby clothes, and how to dress the baby for an outing in the park.

It was really engaging as a mid-century historical artifact. But there was a section called something like "Baby's Day." It was a timeline for what the baby should be doing during the day and what time of day a baby should be given what type of care. It was terrifically detailed and timed out to the minute. It included time in the sun, a time for juice, a time to play alone in their crib, and many other details.

Here was the problem that I noticed with this book: every family is different and every family routine has to suit the individual family and the routines that were laid out in that book only worked for some families. Being very aware of the vast diversity among families, I am not going to map out a timetable and announce that it is ideal for every home. However, I would like to share with you the benefits of having a reliable routine in your home for your family.

Routines that are predictable create a sense of stability in your home. This, in turn, helps keep the kids and adults from feeling unsteady and confused. Living on a wing and a prayer may sound like fun, but it isn't really. Instead, it resembles trying to walk on a trampoline: a lot of work, but very little forward progress.

When there is no routine in place, everyone is faced with the exhausting tasks of planning and anticipating and juggling and rescheduling and forgetting then remembering at the last minute. With a predictable schedule, life runs more smoothly and more is accomplished with less anxiety.

Routines for children are especially helpful and healthy as they pertain to food and sleep. I am very surprised at the number of families that have no set bedtime or mealtimes for the children. Both of these ensure that children are getting what they need to stay healthy physically and emotionally. Routines are a source of security.

I am a strong proponent of making sure that children eat healthy homemade food, but my biggest soapbox issue, and I will talk you into a coma about this, is that children need a bedtime that reflects the number of hours of sleep they require for their age. Young children require a great deal of sleep in order to grow, retain what they learned throughout the day, and maintain healthy emotional levels.

If you haven't gotten a bedtime routine set for your children, I encourage you to get that party started. Begin by deciding a wake-up time in the morning. Sleep experts agree that waking up at the same time each day is the most healthy routine. Then back up from that time and set bedtime about thirty minutes before the number of hours your child needs to sleep each day according to their age. There are many resources for determining that number, but the American Academy of Pediatrics sleep guidelines is easy to find using any internet search engine. You will find an easy-to-follow chart.

As you set up activities for your family, make sure that you are not overbooking yourself or your child. I have taught children's piano lessons during several different seasons of my adult life and I have always been amazed at the number of children that come to me for a lesson immediately after they have left the swim team practice or soccer practice and then leave me to go directly to their karate class or whatever.

Seriously. I had one little girl who would sit week after week on the piano bench yawning and exhausted from the school swim team practice only to get up at the end of the lesson and go to the restroom to change into her clothes for karate. Every week

I heard her tummy grumble. It was six o'clock when she left her lesson with me.

I also taught guitar classes and clearly remember asking one boy if he had practiced and he told me what activity he had each day. There was soccer three days a week; then there were scouts, piano, and swimming on top of that. I have known dozens of children with this kind of schedule. Please leave your children some time to just be.

Routines help everyone. Having a general idea and guidelines for when, what, and where the family is going to be and what they will be doing doesn't mean that there is no room for spontaneity, but it does aid in offering a sense of security.

Summary of Chapter Five

- Roles in a family are there to help everyone function in their area of giftedness as well their area of responsibility. Roles are not assigned to limit anyone's ability to try new things or learn a new role.
- Roles are not a permanent assignment. They are flexible and may change depending on the situation. The one in charge in any given setting should be the one most capable of being in charge.
- Adults should be constantly teaching the children how to take the next step toward adulthood. As your children learn new things, allow them to take on the role of teacher, and you model being the learner
- As you fill your role and help your children to fill their roles, remember that you are not training your helpers; you are training your replacements.

- Rules are a necessary part of any harbor home. They will shift over time and may not always be considered fair.
- Rules apply to different individuals under different circumstances and some will change with maturity
- As rules are established, be aware of your parenting style. Authoritarian, permissive, uninvolved, or authoritative.
- Routines, especially with regard to sleep and food, are a cornerstone to stability and security.

Questions For Discussion or Deeper Thinking

1. What do you think your parenting style is? Why do you classify yourself in that way?
2. After discovering a bit about parenting styles, do you want to change yours? Why or why not?
3. Describe your family's harbormaster and how that person fills this role.
4. When was the last time you let your child teach you something that you did not know? What was it and how well did you learn?
5. How do you feel about your family's current routine? Do you think it needs readjusting?

Chapter Six

THE OCEAN: RIDING OUT THE WIND AND WAVES

Suddenly a furious storm came up on the lake, so that the waves swept over the boat. But Jesus was sleeping. The disciples went and woke him, saying, "Lord, save us! We're going to drown!"

Matthew 8:24–25

Hurricanes and storms are a part of life on Ocracoke Island as they are in all coastal communities. In every category of climate on the earth, there is some sort of naturally occurring danger that can cause havoc for the population.

On Ocracoke storms that vary in strength, size and duration are routinely experienced. Naturally, there are hurricanes. These can last for days and the after-effects can last for years. There are also weather events that are less memorable such as tropical storms or downpours that are caused by low-pressure systems that get stuck in the region and remain until a high-pressure system builds enough strength to push it out.

There are the infamous nor'easters that can cause substantial damage. Sometimes these wreak as much or more havoc than a hurricane. Nor'easters get their name from the direction of the predominant wind throughout the duration of the storm. They are at their most fierce in the winter when it is not hurricane season.

On Ocracoke Island, the residents, as a rule, take these storms in stride. They anticipate them and know what to do to protect their property and themselves to the extent that it is possible. Storms are a natural part of the ebb and flow of life in the village.

Storms come into every harbor home. They may be large or small, they may do damage that lasts a while or they may be easily swept away, but they are a real part of the human condition for everyone. The only thing that we can do is accept this as a fact and learn how to stand strong throughout.

As people of faith, we are offered help and support in the words of the Holy Scriptures. Taken in its entirety the Old and the New Testaments are about people, ordinary and extraordinary, who navigate storms in their culture and personal lives while continuing to trust and rest in the harbor of the Lord.

We read about these experiences of stress and distress and how God's ancient people managed to maintain a life of faith. When we are inundated with grief or confusion we pray and ask God for the strength to overcome hardships as they did.

Or do we? When a stressful situation looms on the horizon or jumps up suddenly with one phone call, what is your first response?

Is it prayer? Or is it anger? Is it fear? Is it determination? Is it calm? Is it courage? Is it full-on panic?

You, like me, have probably responded at different times and in different situations with each of these. But there is a better way to respond in times of crisis, and we can learn it. It is a way that helps us maintain a balance between acceptance and action when we are experiencing storms. It is the way of Christ.

In parish ministry, my husband and I are privileged to walk with individual people and entire families through difficult days and joyous occasions or as they maneuver through their workday lives. We often sit murmuring words of encouragement and comfort while people respond to moments of crisis with a wide range of understandable reactions. Often they say that they wish they were responding better. I assure them that I usually wish I had responded better to a crisis too. Sometimes we only turn to a faith-filled response after every other response leaves us unhealed and unaided.

I want to be like Deborah or her friend Jael and respond to crises with unimaginable strength and courage and faith. (Judges 4–5) I want the Wonder Woman kind of presence that those women had. And you know what? We each have within us the ability to do this. We have this assurance in Philippians 4:13 that *I can do all this through Him who gives me strength.* We can achieve a level of strength and courage that will keep our hearts turned to God because God has given us that ability. We just have to tap into it.

What does this strong and faithful response look like in our daily lives? What practical steps of faith can we take now to set ourselves up to respond to times of distress in a way that we can look back at later and say confidently, "I knew that the Lord was with me and I responded in faith?" Chapter Six will be a discussion of some ways to make your faith such a natural part of your life that you can begin to turn to it without thought or hesitation in times of need.

Your Prayer Life

The phrase "prayer life" is not found in Scripture precisely in those words. It is a term that refers to the personal practices that you and I use to help us pray regularly, pray within God's will, and to turn to prayer at a moment's notice. As you build your prayer life it will become stronger and more natural to you. This happens because when you come near to God, He will come near to you. (James 4:8) And when God comes near amazing and miraculous things begin to happen.

Your faith will grow not because you are being so good and so faithful but because God is so good and so faithful. You don't have to build an impressive vocabulary of Scripture or prayer-like words to elevate your prayer life. Just intentionally draw near to God in a way that is authentically you. Then wait to see what incredible things God will do in your heart.

Developing a deep and abiding prayer life will not, I repeat, will not keep you from experiencing setbacks or hardships or any of the difficulties that come to us all. Prayer is not a shield from harm, it is a shield from defeat.

Faith in Christ does not give anyone a pass from suffering pain or discouragement, but it is the path that we can use to bring us back from our troubles with greater strength and experience that teaches us that God is faithful and true and is involved in our lives.

Christ, who was Himself God, had a deep, rich and faithful prayer life. He prayed alone, He prayed with His friends, He prayed before meals and in the synagogues. He prayed on the road, on hillsides, in boats, on the shore, and in the homes of friends. He prayed for healing, He prayed for peace, He prayed for God's will to be done.

Following this example keeps us in a constant state of prayer. As we pray we are not talking to ourselves, but to the God who created and sustains us. We can, as John describes in the fourth chapter of Revelation, enter the throne room of Heaven and pray to the One who sits on the throne. This is prayer with confidence. Go to God knowing that He hears you and wants you, His precious child, to be whole.

So begin to strengthen your prayer life by praying like Jesus. Pray constantly. Everywhere you go. Pray aloud in your room, pray silently, pray with your friends, pray with your family. Pray with your children. Pray before you eat. Pray at the altar of your church. Pray beside your bed or in your yard. Pray as you work, pray as you walk, pray as you shop, pray as you doze into sleep.

Step one is to follow the example of Jesus and pray in any and all circumstances. Begin to pray now. Pray like no one is watching or listening except God. And know that He loves you and is smiling at you and is with you.

Keep Going

Several years ago, when I was in my early fifties, we were with the family in Hatteras Village on the Outer Banks. Before leaving on this trip I had made a secret promise to myself that while we were there I was going to do something that I had wanted to do for a long time. I knew the family would think it was pretty silly, but I wanted to do it anyway. So I waited until everyone who wasn't fishing was napping. My moment had come. I quietly snuck away from the cottage telling no one.

I wanted to go to Ocracoke Island Village by myself. But that's not all. I wanted to ride my bicycle (a constant companion at the OBX) to get there. You may be wondering right now exactly how I was planning to ride a bicycle to an island. Good question. Well, the plan was that I was going to ride my bike five miles from our rented house in Hatteras, get on the ferry to Ocracoke Island and then ride my bicycle the thirteen miles to the village. Then I was planning to spend an hour or so reveling in my accomplishment. After that, I was going to reverse the process. What could possibly go wrong? I had water in my backpack. I sprayed on insect repellent and put on sunscreen. What else did I need?

It started out quite well. The five-mile ride on NC Hwy 12 in Hatteras was easy. The route is flat and the road is generously wide in order to accommodate bicycles. I am not an athlete but I am pretty active, so I was feeling good. The plan was working.

I arrived at the ferry dock, got in line, and boarded the ferry. There is a spot for bicycles and a lounge for passengers, so I parked my bike and went up the stairs to enjoy the view of the Atlantic Ocean and the Pamlico Sound. The trip was about thirty minutes long back in those days and the weather was beautiful. A brisk breeze was blowing on a perfectly hot summer day. There was not a cloud in the sky and everything was going my way. I felt great.

My bicycle and I got off the ferry and I began to pedal the thirteen miles down the stretch of NC Hwy 12 that continues along Ocracoke Island. It was a truly hot and humid day but I was very enthusiastic. I was crossing off a bucket list item. As I set out, more than a few tourists riding by in their air-conditioned cars looked at me as though I had truly taken leave of my senses. I didn't care. Let them drive their cars! I was traveling by pedal power! I was a free and independent woman of adventure!

It was less than a mile later and I realized that I was hot. Really hot. Overheated kind of hot. Perhaps even dangerously hot. How could this be? I had been fine riding on Hatteras. What was the difference?

I kept my eyes on the road as I pedaled with increasing difficulty. The sun and the heat were relentless and I was beginning to think that perhaps I had missed some essential piece of information. I had. But I didn't figure out what it was until I stopped at the Pony Pasture on the side of the road to take a drink of water.

So that you can understand my predicament, I should tell you that the section of NC Hwy 12 on Ocracoke is a slice of asphalt between the sand dunes on the beach and a maritime forest on the sound side. This forest is made of sugar maples, wild dogwood, juniper, white ash, and other trees. The trees are perfectly adapted to the environment. They grow quite low to the ground here and are constantly windblown so that their trunks are bent over. They can withstand the salt spray thanks to a natural waxy coating on their leaves and they can tolerate flooding. On the part of the island where the Hatteras Ferry docks are, this wooded area stretches to the sound side of the island. It is not wide; perhaps a few hundred yards in some places but it played a vital role that day.

I was traveling south so I looked to my left and saw the sand dunes towering at least twenty feet high in some places. On my right was the dense stand of trees and brush that stretched most of the way to the village. It was these natural barriers that I had forgotten to take into account. The huge dunes and the trees blocked every bit of the wind that had cooled me as I pedaled on Hatteras. There was no refreshing breeze to blow away the heat. None. At all. I could hear the roar of the Atlantic Ocean, but no coastal wind could be felt. Oops. This was a small but important detail.

The breeze which would have kept me cool would have been beneficial in one other way as well. It is well known that the Outer Banks have many famous features. What often goes unmentioned is that among these features are vicious, dive-bombing squadrons of mosquitoes. I am pretty sure that on that day I saw at least one that was approximately the same size as a small house cat. I think they may even fly in formation.

At the Outer Banks the best protection against these pests, other than insect repellent, is the nearly constant breeze that blows from the ocean. Mosquitoes and many other insects are so light that they cannot withstand the wind and so there is usually a natural protection from these pests.

On that day, the wind was blowing from the east and every hint of a refreshing and helpful breeze was blocked by the sand dunes. Not only was the heat oppressive but the moment I stopped pedaling, the mosquitoes began biting me through the insect repellent that rolled off of me as I perspired in the heat. While stopped on the side of the road for just a few moments I was bitten by dozens of mosquitoes and stung by a couple of large flies.

At that moment I realized that I had two choices, but only one good choice. Keep going. As long as I was moving the wind created by the motion kept the insects off of me and provided a little bit of cooling. It was brutally hot, but I knew that I could make the trip to the village in a little over an hour. The next ferry didn't make the trip back to Hatteras for over an hour. Going back was not an option I was going to consider.

I knew that if I rode without stopping until I reached the village, I could take a break on one of the porch swings under the trees where the breeze blows freely virtually every minute. I didn't know if I could make it that far without a break but I decided that I was going to give it all I had.

So that's what I did. I rode on. From time to time I wondered what on earth I was thinking when I thought that this was a good idea. But for most of the ride, I thought almost nothing at all. I pedaled. I kept going. Legs aching, heart pounding, sweat pouring. I stayed the course. Heat, humidity, mosquitoes. Keep pedaling.

I had known from the first moment I had the crazy idea in the first place that it would be a challenge because I am not an avid cyclist. But I simply had not factored in the lack of a breeze. It never crossed my mind. This made this challenge much more difficult than I had imagined or prepared for, but I had wanted to have this little adventure for a long time and I was going to see it through.

Have you ever been in a bad situation? Maybe one of your own making? Something that sounded like a good idea at the time but then there was an element that you hadn't prepared for and suddenly you are in trouble? Most of us have.

Perhaps a second job sounded like a good idea until you found yourself drowning in more work than you planned and that extra paycheck now seems a little less enticing. Or maybe you quit your job before securing another. Or decided to drive your car with an expired license thinking that it would be okay this once and it wasn't.

Many of our difficult situations result from someone failing to plan or not factoring in all details. Sometimes the unpredictable or unimaginable happens and our lives are upended and we are thrown into a time of turmoil. Sometimes we start something and finishing it is going to take more than we sbargained for.

Our fault, someone else's fault, no one's fault, we are still experiencing a storm and we don't like it. What is the one best thing that we can all do during these times? Keep pedaling. Stay the course. Ride on.

Winston Churchill is famous for encouraging the people of wartime Britain to never give up. This is the solution for virtually all the storms we encounter. The easiest thing to do is to quit, but quitting seldom produces a worthwhile result.

Whatever the storm, whatever the challenge, keep going. Keep working to communicate with your frustrated teen. Continue to patiently steer your overactive toddler. Engage positively with your spouse even after a ten or more hour workday. Do your job well in spite of the critical coworker. Keep sending your resume. Keep pitching the idea. You are not guaranteed the exact success you are looking for, but you will, at the very least, succeed at giving it your best. And you will grow stronger.

Perseverance will take you places that talent and skill can't. Perseverance is the trait that will breed happiness and lead you to reach your God-given potential. More challenges are overcome, more goals are reached, more problems are solved, more mountains are moved with perseverance than with anything else. The act of simply hanging in there and pressing on is often the best way to ride out the waves of a storm.

You have choices and one of those is to quit, turn around and go back. Let someone else carry the load to the finish line or just drop it on the side of the road. Let someone else take responsibility for balancing the checkbook, educating the children, caring for the aged one. If you choose this, you will spend the rest of your life making excuses and justifying to yourself why. What you won't have is the satisfaction of making it through the storm and being stronger as a result. Do not give up.

Gradually I got closer to the village that day, and as the road widened, the wind began to blow a little again. A funny thing happened then. I was filled up with excitement. I should have been exhausted, but I wasn't. I was exhilarated. I made it. I did it. I accomplished a bucket list challenge and, as silly as it was, it was important to me. I did not give up even when I was certain that everyone I knew would have encouraged me to do so.

I made it to the village in about an hour and fifteen minutes. I stopped at the first snow cone stand I came to and bought a raspberry snow cone and a large ice water. Both were consumed in record time. My goal was achieved, and I was covered in success. Like a kid who jumped off the high dive for the first time, I was grinning from ear to ear.

I made the rounds of all the sights and all the shops wishing that I had a t-shirt that announced my accomplishment. I wanted someone to ask, "Did you ride your bicycle from the ferry?" so that I could blush modestly and say, "Well, yes. I wasn't very fast but I did make it." No one asked. So I celebrated the goal the same way I achieved it. In my own heart. That's the best way anyway.

Sitting in the shade on a porch swing in front of a shop, I rested and considered why I wanted to ride my bike 36 miles in one day all alone. I suppose it was to prove to myself that I was strong and tenacious and had an adventurous spirit. I believed all these things about myself, but I felt the need to really know it in the heart of my hearts.

Was I all those things? Yes. And I still am. So are you. You may not want to prove it by riding your bike to an island, but you prove it every day by staying the course with your family and your responsibility. Just pedal all the way to the village. The sweat rolls, the mosquitoes bite, your muscles burn but there is a shady porch swing at the end of the journey. Don't give up and hand your burden to another. You can do it.

The trip back to the ferry and Hatteras was difficult, challenging, and jubilant. I was doing it. I was stronger and better and even faster on the return trip. I did not have to question if I could do it, because I knew I could. I got back to the ferry dock just in time to ride up on the ferry like a pro. I greeted the crew like we were old friends and went up to the passenger lounge.

The soft seats and the air conditioning were a very welcome aid to recovery and helped prepared me for the five-mile ride back to our cottage. I made it. I have not ever done that again and, furthermore, have no plans to. But I did it. And you can meet the challenges in your life with the same tools of determination and grit.

As this section of the chapter closes, I want to say that there are some rare exceptions to never giving up. There are a few situations in which giving up is the best and smartest option. This is the most important one: if you are in an abusive marriage or long-term relationship, get out of it. Abusers do not stop being abusive. Get whatever help you need to give up on a marriage that keeps you demoralized, cowed, or frightened. You won't be able to do it on your own but there is help. You can let this go. But in virtually everything else, do as Winston Churchill strongly suggested and never, never, never give up.

Ask For Help

Those of us who were raised in the western cultures of The United States, Canada, Europe, etc. have an individualistic approach to life. We thrive on the idea of individual success and pride ourselves on our ability to get through hard times on our own. We prize those who are "self-made."

Other cultures, notably most Asian and many African cultures, approach life as a community. They give and receive help in good times and bad believing that one person is only as successful as the group. The community goals are more important than those of an individual. An accomplishment by one is not as admired as an accomplishment that was achieved by the entire group.

There are definitely pros and cons to each of these cultural foundations. Neither approach is better, but they are radically different. We could learn a great deal from each other and, in fact, I see evidence in the young people I know that this fusion is beginning.

Perhaps you were raised with either the spoken or unspoken rule that you should not ask for help no matter how much you need it. If this describes you as thoroughly as it describes me, please pay attention. Recovery is available.

Asking for help is as simple as asking for anything else that you need. It is not an admission of defeat or failure but a recognition that you don't know everything. And that is okay. None of us do. Even though your family is doing well, they could be struggling in areas that you haven't seen. Everyone needs help sometimes, and let me say this one more time: it is okay.

The first step in learning to ask for help is to accept that you need help. Once you have done everything you know how to do to fix what is wrong and you still don't have it solved, you need to seek those who can and will offer help. In Ephesians 6:13 we read that once we have done all we can do, we should stand firm. But standing firm doesn't have to mean standing alone. Seek out a lighthouse. (See Chapter Four.) Ask your lighthouse for help. That is what lighthouses do. But you have to ask.

Once you realize that you need help and have identified a lighthouse that can help you, contact your lighthouse. Just tell them what is going on. Explain honestly and completely. Leaving out key information, no matter how embarrassing, will only delay finding a solution. Just say aloud what has gone wrong. No matter what it is.

The next step is to watch and learn and gain experience. Many of life's hiccups repeat themselves. As you and your lighthouse work through the situation make sure that you are learning how to resolve this or a similar issue if it comes around again. Maybe you can learn to avoid it next time.

Learn how to fix your problem well enough to help someone else when you see your neighbor in trouble. Remember that the lighthouse should not solve your problem for you. You must work yourself out of the hole you are in. The lighthouse throws you a line, but you still have to do the climbing.

You may be in a storm of your own making. Many of the storms we face are created by our own hands. It may be a lack of experience or carelessness but we really do make most of our own storms. In that situation, you may be reluctant to find a lighthouse because you know that they know that you got yourself into a mess. They may scold or criticize or ask why you let this happen and what on earth you were thinking.

As painful as it is, this may well be part of the process. Perhaps you need to consider what you were or were not thinking as you drew closer to the situation you are in. Did you see it coming? Should you have? Could you have prevented it from going as far as it did? All these things are part of the strengthening and growing process that will help you become all that God created you to be. We are designed to learn and grow throughout our entire lifetimes but sometimes the learning is hard. Listen with humility if your lighthouse is asking difficult questions.

Notice What Is Going Right

Have I mentioned how much I love my husband? He is the finest man I have ever known. He's smart, well educated, funny, resourceful, loving, compassionate, kind to animals and children, and he loves his mama. He's great. He does one little thing, however, that occasionally drives me to the brink of insanity: he looks on the bright side of everything. Always looking at the glass as half full. Mister positive attitude. How aggravating! Please understand that I am also an optimistic and positive person, but sometimes, if I am upset about something, I can let my thoughts and emotions go south pretty quickly. I'm working on this.

If you are facing a difficult situation that does not have a quick and obvious solution, it is easy to let this affect the way you feel toward your entire life at the moment. Anxiety flows over every surface of your life the way a gallon of milk covers the entire kitchen floor when it is spilled. It can seem that everything is wrong even when in reality most things are fine.

This is when someone like my husband can come in handy. When things go wrong, he immediately begins to count the things that are going right. He doesn't necessarily focus on those things because he is focusing on seeking a solution to the problem, but he notices and mentions the good things.

He remembers that we are children of the Most High God and we are covered in that protection, and he makes sure I get that memo too. As much as I hate to admit it in a moment of distress, I'm so grateful that my husband has that ability. Although I am not as good at it as he is, I have learned so much about how to accomplish this. This is a skill you can learn. Here are a few tips that I have picked up as I have grown in this way.

- **Emotions can lie.**

  Your emotions may be driving your life more than is appropriate. Emotions are there to protect us and nurture us and enhance our lives. But there are some times when it is more prudent to ignore how you feel so that you can concentrate on what you know. When you are feeling as though your entire life is spiraling the drain, remember what you know to be true. Review what is working in your life and write it down if you have to. Connect your heart to your brain. When reason and emotions are working together we have a better perspective on everything.

- **It came to pass.**

  I once read about an elderly lady who was asked what her favorite verse of Scripture was. She immediately responded with, "It came to pass." The people around her were a bit surprised at this and asked her why. She explained that this phrase, used dozens of times in the old and new testaments, reminded her that nothing in life comes to stay. Good times and hard times all pass away. With wisdom, we learn to embrace and appreciate the good times and endure with patience the hard times. They all "come to pass"; they do not "come to stay". This challenging time you are facing will pass. You will get through it. Learn what you can and move forward.

- **Talk to yourself.**

  I talk to myself all the time. I bet you do too. Sometimes I need an expert opinion and so I ask myself for one. This works more often than you might think. But when things are in a jumble and you are worried you need to talk to yourself and remind yourself that everything is going to work out. Find a place to be alone and tell yourself out loud that you are loved and you will be okay. Saying it out loud helps more than just saying it in your head because you are using several paths to get the message to your brain. You have to think it, speak it, and hear it. Three streams each carrying the same message of truth and comfort. It works. Try it.

> There is a great legend about Susanna Wesley, mother to John and Charles Wesley, founders of Methodism, that says that when she needed a moment alone she would put her apron over her face. With all those children and living in a church-owned rectory I suppose that was the only recourse she had. Anyway, this Godly woman often comforted herself by saying aloud the Words of God while hiding beneath her apron. Do what you have to do however you have to do it.

Storms will come along in every life. They may seem insurmountable at the moment but one day you will wake up and realize that things are better than they were yesterday or last week. Gradually the situation is improving. Maybe there will be a solution that presents itself in a moment.

Whatever form healing takes, healing will come. Healing may not look like what you expected or asked for but you will not always be worried or angry or frustrated. The day will arrive when you realize that you are on the other side of whatever it was. You will get through it.

Summary of Chapter Six

Even though the events of our lifetimes are often described as mountains and valleys or highs and lows, I think there's a better description.

I believe the events of our lifetimes are like those old-fashioned car rides that were in amusement parks years ago. The kind where there is a center rail in the track and the car, with a steering wheel that apparently has no function at all, bounces on the inside of the tires from left to right and back again all the way to the end of the ride. Good and bad, joyful and trying, tribulation and triumph. These are always near and we go back and forth between the two rails while moving forward.

There will be times when things go well and times when things are not going as we would like. All of these are in God's hands and are part of His divine plan for our greater good and His ultimate glory.

It is hard to believe during moments of trouble and fear that God is with us and loves us, but this is the promise that we are given over and over. There is no magic wand that will instantly make everything all better, but the assurance that comes from Scripture has strengthened generations of the faithful. It can strengthen you also.

As you are navigating the storms in your home there are ways that you can remain steady and on course. Using these tools will help you get through the difficulties and challenges that are part of each life. In addition, using these tools will build your strength and help you to become an even better and more capable leader of your harbor home.

Focus on strengthening your prayer life by following the prayer practices of Christ. Don't give up. Keep going and moving ahead. Persevere all the way through the challenging times. Notice what is going right and focus on things other than your problem. Keep your emotions under your control rather than allowing your emotions to drive your life. These tools are reliable and are improved with practice. Make them a part of your storm kit.

Questions for Discussion or Deeper Thinking

1. How have you used the tools in this chapter when you have had a deep disappointment such as not getting the job or promotion you wanted and deserved?
2. Describe a time when you were experiencing a storm of your own making and how you got through it. Are you proud of how you responded?
3. What was the greatest lesson you learned from a challenging time?
4. How can you prioritize your emotional responses during a crisis so that they help rather than hinder your healing?
5. What motivates you to keep going when you are experiencing a challenge?

Chapter Seven

HURRICANES: REBUILDING WHEN THE STORM COMES INTO THE HARBOR

I sink in the miry depths where there is no foothold. I have come into deep waters; the floods engulf me.

Psalm 69:2

On the night of September 5, 2019, Hurricane Dorian hit Ocracoke Island with staggering ferocity. The storm itself moved through quickly, but at approximately 7:30 on the morning of September 6, a storm surge of over seven feet washed across the island covering it in water from the Pamlico Sound. This level of floodwaters had not been seen since 1944. The village was devastated. Homes were flooded and businesses destroyed in two hours.

The forecast had not been all that alarming as Dorian made its way up the east coast of the United States. Although it had been a devastating category five hurricane when it went through the Bahamas, it was "only" a category one when it drew near the Outer Banks of North Carolina (NC). But a category one hurricane still is a dangerous storm and can cause other serious situations that are more difficult to predict, such as storm surge. It was really these secondary effects that brought such wreckage to Ocracoke.

A very large section of NC Hwy 12, the only road that leads to the Hatteras Ferry and the fastest path to higher ground, buckled and was ripped apart. Much of the rest of that road was covered in feet of sand. Some of the residents of Ocracoke had to be airlifted to safety from the roofs of their homes. Nearly every car on the island was flooded and Ocracoke Village, whose economy is based on tourism, was closed for business. No one could predict how long it would take to recover. As of the summer of 2021, the damage left behind by Dorian was still evident.

Six months after Hurricane Dorian struck and the people of Ocracoke were working to prepare for the summer season of 2020 the entire world, including this tiny island, was hit with another storm in the form of COVID-19. This one-two punch was stunning. How would they ever come back from this loss? Could they ever come back from this loss?

They could and they would come back, but Ocracoke would be a slightly different place moving forward. Some things would have to change. Compromises would have to be made. Strength and courage had to be found and utilized. It was hard. Recovery from devastating loss is never easy nor do we ever get back to exactly where we were before. But we can come back. We can recover and we can live again.

On Ocracoke Island in the months following Dorian, the work began on the homes and shops. They had to be raised and placed on stilts to avoid being flooded in this manner again. While newer construction was already built to stand above floodwaters the older historic homes, some dating back to the nineteenth century, were still quite low to the ground and were badly damaged by the flooding.

The flooded properties included the United Methodist Church in the village. This historic building had to be raised and rebuilt if it was to be saved, and so the process began. Money and volunteers came in and they worked together to resurrect this sacred space.

One little glitch, however, was that raising the church building elevated the steeple to a height that exceeded the maximum allowed by the Ocracoke Development Ordinance. Hyde County, NC council met on February 11, 2020 and passed an amendment to this ordinance that added church steeples to the list of structural accessories, similar to antennae, that could be higher than this maximum. Compromise. Change. Readjustments. Recovery.

Many families have experienced devastation that changes them forever. In our vocations, my husband and I have borne witness to so many of these heartbreaking events, and have seen the far-reaching and life-changing effects. But along with that, we have also borne witness to the incredible resilience of the human spirit and how people manage to recover and find restoration after the worst day of their lives.

Chapter Seven is a tribute to individuals and families that I have known across the decades who have been devastated more than most of us ever experience. These are the bravest people I have ever known. They each, in their own way, are more than survivors;

they are thrivers. I am protecting their identities by merging some details and changing others. The core of these stories, including the events that took place, is true.

We Used to Have a Sister

Their local elementary school was and is a rare gem. A small school in which everyone knows each other, it remains a center of community life. Science fairs, reading clubs, carnivals, field days, and more are events that are well attended by the students and their families. That day was no exception. The school gym was full of excited students and proud parents and grandparents. Friends and neighbors talked and laughed about their children, shared local gossip, and made plans for later that evening.

Our young friends, a delightful couple we had known casually for years, had driven to the school event separately that day. The stepdad was on his motorcycle, having gone to the school event straight from work, while the mom and all three children left their house and went to the school in the small family car. After the event ended, the family headed home.

Stepdad went ahead on the bike, and at an intersection not far from the school the mom and children were hit by a car that ran a stop sign. Both cars were wrecked on the shoulder of the rural highway. Our friend took all three of the children, unharmed, out of their car seats and they all stood on the side of the road while they waited for the state patrol to come.

The driver of the other car decided to try to move her vehicle and found that it was stuck fast where it landed. She got out of the car leaving it running. Suddenly the car jerked and, with no one in control, it lunged in a narrow arc hitting and instantly killing the precious only daughter of this young mother. It happened in a flash. Immediately after the impact, their only car caught fire and was completely destroyed.

The stepdad had begun to wonder where the rest of his group was and turned around just in time to see the flames and to find out that their lives had just stopped. In vain he tried to rescue the child. They lost the little girl that day. To say that they were devastated is to completely understate the situation.

We were notified of this incident early the next day. We immediately dropped everything else and drove to their community to see how we could help. The family could not wrap their minds around the loss and did not want a funeral. Instead, we had a gathering of friends at a local funeral home. No one spoke, there was no music.

The surviving siblings saw me arrive and, recognizing me, came to speak. One of them immediately asked me if I knew that they had been in a car wreck. I responded that I did know. His next words left me floored. "We used to have a sister," he said. I nodded because words failed me. I hugged them and listened to them for a long time that evening, and then everybody went home.

Their story was on the news for a few days, and someone who saw the story gave them a car since they only had the small motorcycle for transportation. Individuals and churches donated money in a desperate attempt to show love to this young family. It was harrowing, and for several weeks we lost touch with them.

But one day a few months later we got a call. It was the stepdad. He wanted my husband to officiate the marriage between him and the woman he loved. He loved her and the children he declared. In addition to marrying this woman, he was working through the process of adopting the surviving children. He was no longer willing to be the stepdad, he wanted to be the dad. He wanted the family to be whole in every way they possibly could be.

In the time of greatest grief, this family found the beginnings of healing through commitment and unity. The wedding, held in our backyard, was sweet and private. The tiny urn holding the remains of the one they lost was placed on a makeshift altar as they pledged to be a family from that day forward. And they were. And they are. The other children were legally adopted and for several years now they have called that man Daddy.

In the years since the accident that changed their lives, their social media pictures have shown a happy family that overcame horrific loss through forming and strengthening bonds. We have spent Thanksgiving with them a few times and are touched by the depth of their love and care for one another. How we admire and love them.

Although a hurricane came into this family's harbor home and brought catastrophic destruction, they were able, in time and with a commitment to one another, to rebuild a harbor that continues to shelter and sustain them.

They remain dear friends and a family that we are close to. Each year they remember the sweet life gone too soon, but they have found joy in the life that remains. Commitment. Holding on to what remains. Rebuilding the harbor.

A Shining New Life

In December of 2007, I was offered an exciting new ministry opportunity and I was thrilled. Even though I was sorry to be leaving the children I loved where I was, this new offer was my dream job and I accepted it. On an unseasonably warm day, I dressed in baggy sweatpants, an equally baggy sweatshirt, and with my hair covered in a paint-splattered bandana, I went to clean out the office I was vacating.

While I was in the parking lot trying to fit boxes of books and games in my car, the office administrator stepped outside. She asked if there was any way to contact my husband that day. I replied that I was sorry, but there was not. He was in a closed meeting of a board that reviews and assesses candidates for ordination. He was over an hour away with his phone turned off.

The administrator explained to me the phone call she had just received. It was from the husband of a couple I had known well when their oldest child, a precious little boy, had been in my pre-kindergarten class a few years earlier. They had moved away from our immediate community and we had not seen them for some time.

The husband, out of town on business and trying hard to get home, called the church and asked for a minister to go sit with his wife at the hospital. She was giving birth to their still-born child, and she was alone.

At thirty-nine weeks of gestation, this precious life was just days away from sleeping in the cradle that had been prepared for him. And suddenly this happened. The shock and grief were complete. This was a deeply loved and desperately wanted third child. It was another little boy that was to have provided their middle daughter with bookend brothers. They had been so excited, and this loss was a lightning bolt out of the blue.

I was the closest thing to a minister we had to offer that day, so without stopping to change out of my grungy clothes I went to the hospital. I prayed every moment of the way asking God to tell me what to do or what to say. I am an early childhood teacher and a Christian educator. That is far from being a pastor or a minister to adults with adult griefs and problems. I felt so incapable.

I arrived at the hospital and sat by the bed of this strikingly pretty woman. She had been given a nerve block so that she would not feel any pain, but she was still quite a few hours away from giving birth. We sat there together talking quietly about what had happened and how she had found out what was wrong. I asked about the other two children who were with friends for the day. We talked throughout the rest of the morning and into the afternoon about things important and trivial.

Shortly after lunchtime, the grandparents of the infant came in. They were grieving but staying strong for their daughter. As I got up to leave so that they could have some privacy, the sweet young mother asked me for a favor.

"Can we baptize him after he is born?" she asked.

"Of course we can," I responded, not really knowing if we could or not. I mentioned that I even had some water from the Jordan River that I had collected, and I would go and get it and come back.

I left the family alone to cry. I got in my car to cry. I did not know the church's position on the baptism of dead infants but I did not care one bit. The opinions of theologians could not have mattered less to me at that moment. I clung to 1 Corinthians 16:14. *Let all you do be done in love.* I would baptize that baby in love. By myself if necessary. No matter what anyone said or thought. Just do the loving thing without overthinking it.

And so the day went on and on. I was finally able to get hold of my husband, and shortly after the baby was born he and I both arrived back at the hospital. Jordan River water was applied to the little head and we all prayed and cried together as we baptized him in love.

By then their entire family, including the baby's grief-stricken father, had gathered in the tiny room and we stepped out to let them finish this moment in privacy. We assured them that we were available anytime. We went home broken-hearted for this family.

Four weeks later, a group of family and friends gathered around the century-old altar in the church sanctuary to commemorate the life that none of us got to share. It was a beautiful service. There was laughter, tears, and a strong acknowledgment that a loss had been suffered. Many people took a turn to speak words of encouragement.

There was a vacancy in this family that would exist forever. But in the midst of all the expressions of grief and love, there was the ever-present awareness that life would go on. Where there is love there is life. Where there is life there is hope.

Eighteen months later, this family celebrated the birth of a beautiful baby daughter whose curly hair and bright blue eyes were the highlight of every family photograph. The years have passed and this family continues to remember the little boy they lost while celebrating the children they have. They faced their grief head-on. They faced it together. No one denied or tried to diminish the loss. They looked loss straight in the eye and believed that they would get through it. And they did.

The little boy who was in my pre-kindergarten class is now a grown man serving in the military. We are thankful for this.

The middle girl has graduated college and is beginning a fine and satisfying career. And the baby girl, who came just in time, is busy in high school dreaming big dreams for her life.

The parents are justifiably proud of all their children. The loss is still recognized each year, but they have all thrived. They faced the worst day of their lives with candor and truth and hope and they came through it stronger than ever. Face tragedy. Don't flinch. Look it in the eye and call it by name.

Healing That Works

The tiny older lady looked like the next wind gust would blow her completely away. Her hair and makeup were flawless and her clothes were very fashionable. Her accessories were funky and yet classic. She was beautiful. As someone who never can seem to really pull an outfit together, I was very impressed by her presentation.

It was hard to judge how old she was because although physically she appeared to be at least fifteen years older than me, her spirit was youthful and joyful. She always had a funny comment to make about things and she was always smiling. She loved her dogs and was passionate about her grandchildren.

We met her on the first day we arrived at a new church appointment. We were moving into a new house in a new community and we were to begin serving the congregation that this woman was part of. She had taken up several leadership roles in the service of this church, and we saw a good bit of her. Especially in those first days.

She prayed with us and for us and made it her mission to help us be comfortable and feel welcome in our new home and church. Her hospitality combined with her knowledge of the community and the congregation helped us immeasurably as we began to settle in. I wanted to know her better. She was clearly a wonderful woman.

It would be easier to describe what this woman didn't do at the church than to describe what she did do. She took the older folks to their doctor appointments or cancer treatments, she played the piano, she taught Sunday school, she baked brownies, and contributed money for the children. She was on several administrative committees and was the voice of reason and calm when opinions differed among individuals. She worked nearly as many hours each week as the paid staff did, and she did with a joyful spirit. She was tireless in her efforts and generosity.

I began to get to know her by simply asking about the brooches that she wore every single day. Her other accessories changed, but I noticed that she was never seen without the same four pins that she put on each day in addition. I wondered what they meant to her. So I asked.

"This one," she began while pointing, "is for my granddaughter, this one is for the granddaughter I adopted, this one is for my daughter, and this one is for my daughter who died."

"Oh," I said. "I'm so sorry. I had no idea." A thousand thoughts ran through my mind and they all led me to think to myself, *but she seems so happy . . . how can this be?*

She told me a very short and simple story that summed up the day her whole world changed. Her daughter, a beautiful and talented girl, was away at college, and while demonstrating on stage an acting technique to a group of younger students she simply collapsed and died. From one moment to the next, with no warning or symptoms or hint that anything was wrong, this lovely girl passed from life to death. Her parents were beyond devastated. Her sister was as well.

But that was not the whole story. At the time of her daughter's death, her husband was in the final weeks of life due to the cancer that he had been fighting like a hero for several years. Ten weeks after her daughter was buried, our friend went back to the funeral home to make arrangements for her husband's memorial service. She recalled to me that she hardly knew that she was putting one foot in front of the other. I was awestruck.

"How did you get through it?" I asked. "You're so joyful. I admire your spirit so much and you have helped us more than you can possibly know. How did you go from that loss to this spirit?" I really wanted to know the secret. I wanted to learn about the strength that would allow a woman to bury her daughter and her husband and rise up again to become an example to many.

She smiled and said that the first thing she did was to create an endowment that would create a scholarship in her daughter's name to the college she was attending. She wanted to help other students. With that accomplished and running smoothly, she moved back home to the community where she now was living. She joined the church and became an integral part of the congregation.

"And now," she said simply, "I work for the Lord. Every day. Everyone I help, every act of service I offer heals me a little more. It has been many years, and I will never be the same, but I am healed through the joy of serving others who are hurting."

It was that simple. There was nothing complicated or inexplicable. She reached out with love to those who needed love and she discovered that the healing she poured out rebounded on her own broken heart. Generous work is a balm for the brokenhearted.

Focus on the needs of others and you will find that one of life's great paradoxes is that the more you give, the more you receive. Healing through serving. Healing works. Working heals. Giving to others those things of the spirit that you yourself need. A beautiful and mysterious truth.

Rebuilding Your Own Harbor

Each of these stories touched my husband and me personally. Although my husband and I have never experienced pain or loss that can even come close to that which we witnessed, we were strongly affected by the experience of standing with them as their harbors were destroyed. We would never say to these friends that we know how they or anyone in these situations feel. Because we don't.

We watched and prayed and did what we could do as people we cared about were knocked flat and stood back up again. They will all say that they did not stand back up on their own. They had help and support from family and friends, strangers, and God. This is part of why we live as a community. When the hurricane comes into the harbor and wipes out all in its path, recovery is a long-term project that requires many helpers.

We have seen people laugh again, find joy again, and live and work and play again, even after the worst thing that can happen happens. You can do this too. So can I. Strength and support and recovery strategies are available to all of us. It is not simple nor is it easy to come back from tragedy. It doesn't happen quickly or without a fair amount of backsliding. Tears and grief too great for words will always be part of life in the harbor, but healing comes. You will be better.

We have learned by watching others how a harbor home can be rebuilt after a disaster. How the people can be restored. Each of these stories represents those who lifted their harbor out of the floodwaters and put the structures on stilts. They cleared away debris, strengthened foundations, and rebuilt.

None of them wanted to have to do this. Each began the work while their hearts were still heavy with grief, but they still recreated a harbor with a cove, a lighthouse, an inlet, routines, and workers. The ocean and its waves are still there, but the cove in their harbor is safe and solid once more

Each of these families used the tools they were given by God in the moment. They grasped the tools and put them to work. If you ever experience a loss so complete that you are left with only wreckage to work with, God will provide you with a tool to rebuild. He will also give you the strength to use it so that you can begin again.

You may find that you rebuild by offering greater commitment and by binding yourself even closer to your home and the ones you love. Drawing nearer, renewing old promises and making them stronger.

Perhaps you will rebuild by facing the worst moments head-on and refusing to try to sweep them away in order to avoid dealing with the pain. You may courageously rise up and look this moment in the eye and make it a part of your story.

You may discover the miracle of healing yourself by offering healing to others who are suffering. Allowing the pain that broke your own heart to become the strength you offer to heal another heart. The mystery of healing yourself by healing others is a beautiful tool that could only have been invented by God our Creator.

Ocracoke Island is looking a lot better than I thought it would these days. Even so, there are still, in the summer of 2021, large amounts of construction material and equipment parked near the United Methodist Church. There are many people who are still working on the rebuilding projects that are still waiting to be completed.

NC Hwy. 12 has been fully repaired and is open to cars and cyclists. You can rent and drive a golf cart or a motor scooter in the village if you want to. The lighthouse still stands, the ferries are running on schedule and school is back in session. The school baseball team is competing against the team from Hatteras next week. It's a home game for the Ocracoke Dolphins. The field is ready for play.

Most of the restaurants and shops have reopened, but not all. Our favorite waterfront eatery by the dock is still abandoned, but they are working toward a comeback. Crafts, music, and art are being created here by the artists that call this island home and things are getting back to normal. Whatever that is.

It is beautiful and quirky and different and historic. It's one of my favorite places to have a coffee or read a book or ride a bike. This small village really is Ocracoke strong. There is a brightly colored hand-painted sign nailed to a tree in the village that says clearly: Ocracoke>Dorian. It is the truth.

So are you. You are Ocracoke strong. You are strong with the strength of Christ. When a hurricane enters your harbor and all seems lost, remember that you yourself are not lost. You are still held in the palm of God's almighty hand. He will give you just the tool you need to rebuild and recover. You will be restored. That is a promise.

Summary of Chapter Seven

Hurricanes are dangerous storms that go wherever they please. They do not care how snug your harbor home is or how well things have been going for you. They can, at any time, hit your harbor and leave behind piles of debris and destruction as far as the eye can see. Every harbor home is susceptible to this kind of devastating event.

We looked at three different families whose experience with tragedy touched many people as they rebuilt their life from the ashes of tragedy. Using the tools that God gave them, they repaired their harbors using a strength that came when they least expected it.

In times of deep loss, God may send you a clear sign that you must bind yourself to those you love even more closely than you ever have before. He may lead you to step forward and claim the role that He has prepared for you so that you and your family can heal and grow together. As the years go by these bonds will strengthen all around you.

God can give you the strength to look at your tragedy without fear or denial. This is not something that is easy to do, but healing requires this very important step. God's gift of clear vision provides a way to move forward in spite of grief and sorrow. Do not turn away from your community at this time. Allow them to come alongside you and love you and grieve with you as you begin to recover your hope and rebuild the harbor.

As you are becoming whole again, offering acts of love and kindness to those who are hurting around you has a tremendous positive impact on your healing. Kindness and generosity will rebound on your own broken heart as other broken hearts are helped through those acts. This is a great mystery that many have discovered.

Recovery from disaster is not easy or quick but it happens. You will regain your strength and the joy of living even after the hurricane has come and gone.

Questions For Discussion or Deeper Thinking

1. Think about the worst day of your life. How have you recovered from it? What tools did you use?
2. How can you encourage someone in your community and help them be restored after a time of devastating loss?
3. What is the greatest ability you have that you can use in service to your community? Have you made a plan to do this?
4. Who in your life needs you to draw nearer to them? How can you do this?
5. What great hurt in your life have you swept under the rug thinking that it would go away? Will you dare to look at it courageously and begin to let it be healed?

THE TIME OUT TECHNIQUE THAT WORKS

Sometimes in a challenging moment, it helps for children (and adults) to hit the reset button. Sometimes we call this "Time Out."

"Time Out" can be a loving and useful technique that allows your child to rein in emotions that have gone spinning out of control. These high emotions are frightening to children and they want to regain their balance, but they often need your help to do so.

I have heard from many parents and teachers of young children and they say to me in frustration, "I've tried time out and it doesn't work!" If this is something that you have said, let me encourage you to try the steps outlined here. Just sending a child to time out because you are frustrated will not give the desired outcome. In fact, this just exacerbates the problem. There is a better way.

Do not skip or skimp on any of these steps. Do this exactly as laid out here and see how well it helps your child and you deal with a situation that seems out of control.

1. Establish ahead of time a quiet, stimulus-free area in your home that is out of the general flow of traffic, but not truly isolated. A small chair could be placed there.
2. Decide what your criteria will be for sending a child to this quiet zone. Unpredictable and arbitrary banishment to timeout is counterproductive. Make sure that you and your children understand, when all is calm, when and for what reasons timeout will be used.
3. When it is time to make use of this space, tell your child that they must go and sit in the quiet area. They should be there for no longer than one minute for each year of age. Walk them there. Tell your child firmly exactly what behavior they displayed that led to them being put here. For example: "You spit at Mommy. In our family, we do not spit, ever. You sit here for three minutes, and then you come to see me."
4. Set a timer for three minutes. Ideally, the child will be able to hear the timer alert when it is done. Important tip: The timer does not begin until the child is quietly seated. While the child is in timeout avoid all conversation.
5. When the timer goes off, speak to the child and ask them to tell you why they needed to sit out. When they do that, tell them that they should say they are sorry. Give hugs and forgiveness and go back to normal activities.

I know this seems ridiculously simple but there are a few keys in this technique that are often overlooked.

- **First:** parents often "send" a child to timeout. It is important to "take" your child to timeout.
- **Second:** parents have timeouts that last too long. Children have short attention spans. One minute for each year of age.
- **Third:** The timer is important and non-optional for this technique.
- **Fourth:** Parents continue to argue with their child about the behavior that occurred. Let conversations end until after the timer goes off.
- **Fifth:** Remember to state the specific behavior that needs to be checked.

Timeout, when used appropriately, is a useful tool for over-stimulated children or children who need help controlling impulses. Try these steps before giving up.

A BEDTIME ROUTINE THAT WORKS

Having a consistent bedtime is a healthy habit for children and adults. Adults know this, but children typically resist the concept of going to bed. This can be a serious power struggle between parents and children. A familiar and consistent bedtime routine helps your children get the rest they need to be healthy.

Try these steps to a low conflict bedtime:

1. Pajamas, teeth brushed, bath, and whatever should be completed.
2. Wind-down time: Thirty minutes or so before bedtime, turn off screens and dim the lighting. Lower the volume of music and voices. This is a great time to read aloud.
3. At the appointed time, everybody gets into their bed with all the cuddly animals, blankets, etc. that they want. This is a good prayer and lullaby time.
4. A drink of water or an extra trip to the bathroom is fine now.
5. "I love you." "Good night." "Sleep tight." And walk away.

The first time the child gets up, take them back to bed while saying "It is bedtime. Good night, I love you. You must stay in bed."

The second and any subsequent times the child gets up, take them back to bed immediately with no conversation at all. Do not respond to questions or complaints. Persevere.

Follow all the steps. Like the timeout routine, it would be easy to skip the key elements. Step seven seems to be the one that parents are most likely to skip. Don't.

ABOUT THE AUTHOR

Teresa Auten is an early childhood specialist with a Bachelor in Science in Early Childhood Development. With over twenty years of experience as a Christian educator focusing on children and youth ministry, Teresa has spent a great deal of time with families as they worked to create the loving, peaceful home that they imagined. Teresa has written articles on the topic of Christian parenting in *Focus On The Family* magazine and a workbook for middle school faith development. She and her husband, Rick, a United Methodist minister, live in Denver, North Carolina on the peaceful shores of Lake Norman. Teresa enjoys doing science experiments with her grandchildren and making music for the Lord. Visit her website at www.joyfulharborhome.com.